The changing face of BEAUTY

ON THE TITLE-PAGE OVERLEAF

The Three Graces

(*above*) fresco from Pompeii,
Raphael, Dürer, Rubens
(*below*) Boucher, Renoir, Picasso

The changing face of

BEAUTY

Four thousand years of beautiful women

Madge Garland

M. BARROWS AND COMPANY, INC: NEW YORK 1957

Contents

Introduction

3000 BC

The story begins with a waist; and this, the earliest symbol of beauty, persists with only occasional lapses throughout recorded history. Small waists, round bosoms, large eyes and curly hair, these are the most important and oft-recurring elements. Although the emphasis shifts and details vary widely, these elements appear again and again. In turn the interest is concentrated on different features and different parts of the body: mouths are sometimes exaggerated, sometimes small; for a century ears vanish and feet are not visible; sometimes all women appear to be seen in the round, at others pointed faces and long necks are à la mode. The large eye was never more admired than under the early Egyptian dynasties, and it has returned to favour with the doe-eyes of to-day. Blondes are perennial, and the preoccupation with hair, its curling, brushing, braiding or close-cropping, reappears again and again. Social taboos change with the years and what may be exposed in one generation is carefully covered in another. Some periods admire a large voluptuous woman while others lay great stress on a slender figure, and it is difficult for the diet-conscious girl of to-day to realise that once upon a time large bosoms and wide hips were popular and that vital statistics were of no account.

In every instance the pictures in this book are taken from contemporary sources. They attempt to give some record of what has been admired during the last 3,500 years. Many obvious and well-known beauties are included, as well as many lesser known who may not perhaps appear beautiful to us. But it is the taste of their time rather than our own with which we are concerned. Sometimes contemporary letters and memoirs have been a guide and portraits of the women spoken of with admiration included. Sometimes the taste of a

AD 1000

king is widely publicised and sets a fashion, and sometimes a painter records with unusual felicity the women he loves. Art is always in advance of nature, and again

AD 1889

and again an artist conceives a new type of woman which a later generation copies.

A hundred years ago photography enters the field but does not make much impact until this century when art begins to abandon the human figure. Portraiture continues with diminishing enthusiasm and the nude vanishes from the scene almost as completely as it did in medieval days. In many points history has come full circle, once again we admire the tiny waist, the fine bust, the doe-eyes. Our one newcomer is the "casual" girl. And will she in her turn be deposed? Will the "lady" make her come-back? What comes next?

7

A Pagan World

This mysterious head known as the "Lady of Elche" was found in Spain near a temple of Artemis and is probably of Graeco-Phoenician origin. Her jewellery bears a striking resemblance to some found on the site of ancient Troy.

In the bright light of the Aegean the earliest known civilization in Europe states clearly what were — and still are — the hallmarks of beauty: tiny waists, splendid bosoms and curly hair. Here in Crete at the very beginning of Western history, every artifice known to future ages is used to accentuate them and the coquetry of the Minoan women appears more closely akin to the sophisticated eighteenth and nineteenth centuries than to the austere splendour of their contemporaries, the Egyptians, or to the classic age of Greece which follows them some thousand years later.

Across the stepping stones of the Greek islands which lead to the shores of Europe come many Oriental influences: the Syrian Astarte's cult of the breasts; the accentuated and elongated eye, so typical of the Egyptians; perhaps the enigmatic smiles of the Etruscans; certainly the magnificent and elaborate jewellery which from earliest days decorates the necks and ears.

8

With the development of Greek art the sculptor creates a type of beauty which has never been excelled: for centuries the measurements and features of the antique Kore and classic Venus are accepted as perfection and ensuing civilizations have created nothing more exquisite than these lovely goddesses, unselfconscious in their nakedness. They have natural figures, firm and well-developed; their waists unlike those of their Minoan forebears are not constricted; their breasts are set high and far apart; and their arms and legs are long, with finely turned wrists and ankles. Feet are now visible, strong and agile – for Greek women walk barefoot or are shod with heel-less sandals. Their features are straight, the fore-head and nose in one unbroken line, and no maquillage is suggested. The eyes are unaccentuated, the long hair waved but no longer elaborately curled. Few contrivances of fashion are admitted but the simplicity of their garments does not prevent them achieving a variety of exquisite effects, as the charming Tanagra figures effectively illustrate.

Freedom from fashion is equalled by freedom in sex; the pregnant girl could claim that Zeus had seduced her on a moun-tainside when her partner might have been a youthful shepherd – and what would have been a bastard in other circumstances became the son of a god in ancient Greece. Naked boys and girls run races and take part in outdoor sports together; and the healthy physique and well-developed limbs of the Greek girls, as well as their exiguous garments, bear a striking resemblance to those of the girls of the twentieth century.

Crete 3,500 years ago

when curled hair, painted eyes
and elaborate jewellery formed part
of every woman's toilette

*A civilisation far older than Greece inspired these
fascinating figures with their protruding breasts, tiny
waists controlled by corsets, and crinoline skirts.*

The large doe-eyes of this pretty dancer from a Cretan fresco
are heavily outlined and her mouth is painted, her hair curled.

Fresh from the hands of
the hairdresser this lady wears
an elaborately embroidered bolero.

*This sophisticated world, full of gaiety and gossip,
essentially feminine and very fashionable, remained
unknown for thousands of years until it was
discovered at the beginning of the century by
Sir Arthur Evans. "Mais, ce sont des Parisiennes,"
was the astonished cry of a learned professor
when he was first shown, in 1900, these frescoes of
Minoan court ladies. They were unlike
anything known in the ancient world
—unlike Babylonians, Egyptians, Greeks—but not
unlike the elaborately corseted and coiffured ladies
of his time. For like Edwardian beauties,
these Cretan women had curled hair and painted faces
and wore clothes of elaborate cut
and brilliant colours.*

10

These frescoes were restored by the Swiss painter Gillieron and placed as nearly as possible in their original positions. The ladies gaily chit-chatting together are wearing complicated coiffures and patterned dresses in delicate shades of blue, green and russet with sleeved bodices which reveal their naked breasts.

Minoan Figurines

with crinoline skirts
and corseted waists

The goddess figure wears the dress of the Minoan court lady with tight-waisted bodice, naked breasts and a crown. In her hands she holds a pair of sacred snakes.

This small wooden figure with upraised arms, known to archaeologists as Our Lady of Sports, wears a golden breastplate, stomacher and cap of intricate workmanship.

12

These exquisite little statues in pottery show the curious curved apron and high, conical hats fashionable in Crete. The Fitzwilliam goddess (*right*) draws attention to her breasts, which were usually exposed and probably a fertility symbol.

13

The importance of the bosom is clearly indicated in this limestone figure of a goddess carved in relief, about 660 B.C. Her curled fringe escapes beneath her head-dress and she has a necklace of beads around her throat.

Egypt

An immense brooding calm lies over this mysterious land. Gaudy colours and patterns are left to barbarians, while men and women alike wear plain white robes, only their jewellery showing richness of decoration. Hair is entirely hidden either by strangely shaped head-dresses or by huge curled wigs. Interest is centred on the eyes which are artificially elongated by painted lines and accentuated by heavy eyebrows.

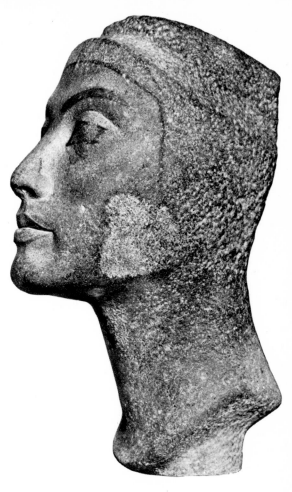

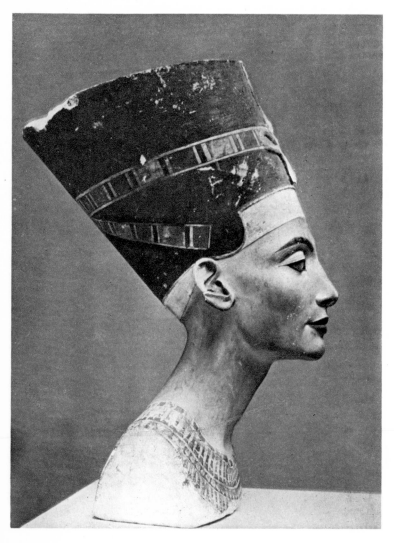

Nefertiti is the first great beauty whose name is known the world over and these two portraits prove her to have been as exquisite as legend recounts. She was the wife of her brother the great Pharaoh Akhenaton, whose features are also of a rare distinction—perhaps the royal couple were lucky in the artists who recorded them? Nefertiti's perfect profile understandably caused a great sensation when these two heads were unearthed in the early years of this century. The famous painted stone head (*left*) was hidden during the war in a salt-mine in Germany, but it has now been safely returned to West Berlin.

(*above*) This elaborate coiffure of frizzed hair held on by a wreath of lotus leaves belongs to the wife of the Pharaoh Rameses' brother. Her eyes are accentuated by heavy maquillage.

(*right*) In this painted limestone statue from her mortuary temple at Deir el Bahri Queen Hatshepsut wears the white crown of Upper Egypt.

Women of
Ancient Greece

(*above*) An early fifth century relief known as "The Throne of Venus" shows the goddess arising from the sea, assisted by two bending handmaidens. She has waved hair held by a fillet, and appears not entirely naked but with a gossamer-fine garment clinging to her wide-apart breasts and firm body.

(*right*) This handmaiden from the Acropolis has long crimped hair similar to that worn by the Minoans. Her face has a broad brow, well sculptured mouth, and the forehead and nose in one unbroken line typical of classic Greek beauty.

18

Long carefully waved hair
frames broad brows and large
widely spaced eyes

(*above*) Aspasia, mistress of Pericles, was celebrated in the fifth century B.C. for her beauty and wit, and the most distinguished men of her time, particularly Socrates, frequented her house. Her name, like that of Egeria, has become synonymous with a wise and secret counsellor.

(*left*) This exquisite kneeling Venus from the island of Rhodes is shown in a pose often copied by sculptors of later periods. She smiles slightly and holds out her long curled hair to dry.

Greek
Perfection

(*above*) This Aphrodite from Cyprus appears to be stepping out of her bath, her hair tied up in a turban. The statue was found in 1901 by a villager on the shore near where, according to legend, the goddess rose from the sea.

(*right*) Phryne, the mistress and inspiration of Praxiteles, one of the greatest Greek sculptors, modelled for many of his works. She sat for this head of Aphrodite when she was very young.

Harmony of mind and body is
implicit in the classic restraint,
perfect proportions and pure profiles of
these statues of goddesses and women

(*above*) The proportions of the Venus de Milo, the most
famous of all classical statues, are considered to set a standard
of ideal perfection and to represent all that is best in Greek art.
She dates from 100 B.C. but was not rediscovered until 1820.

(*left*) Another marble head of Phryne by Praxiteles is thought
to have been executed when her gentle beauty, with deeply
sculptured mouth and dimpled chin, was in its full maturity.

The Mysterious Etruscans

(*above left*) A terracotta head of a young woman with straight classic nose and full lips is covered by what appears to be a jewelled or embroidered hat. Note her long drop ear-rings.

(*above*) An exceptionally graceful little figure of a girl putting on her shoe. She has a long slender neck and her head is tied up in a sort of turban.

(*left*) This enchanting small figurine of a woman doing her hair is one of the earliest examples of a favourite theme of artists throughout the ages.

22

This ancient people from central Italy had an
unconventional sense for the baroque and the fantastic.
In their intriguing figurines the women appear
smiling and gay, with curled hair,
elaborate head-dresses and heavily made up eyes,
and the profusion of jewellery found in their tombs
proves them to have been much cherished.

(*above*) A painted terracotta head with remarkable stylised
eyes and hair has heavily drawn eyebrows and an enigmatic expression. A flower is tucked behind the right ear.

(*left*) This smiling face is painted on a pottery jug. It has a
full mouth and wide-apart eyes set beneath arching brows and
the outline of the curled hair is strongly marked.

Feminine Attitudes

in the
Mediterranean World
circa 300 B.C.

(*above and left*) These two charming groups of girls gossiping together come from Asia Minor. Their draperies still show traces of the original pale pink and mauve colouring.

(*right*) These exquisite little figures from Tanagra in Greece are of ladies amply draped, their hair in curls or wearing pointed sun hats and carrying palm fans.

(*right*) Two unexpectedly individual portraits of a mother and daughter come from a gravestone in Sardinia. Both graceful and smiling women have their long hair caught up in a chignon, a fashion which has reappeared intermittently to the present day.

Roman Matrons

(*above*) Agrippina minor, a ruthless and ambitious woman in spite of her calm face and pretty curls, was the mother of Nero, whom she placed on the throne after murdering her husband, the Emperor Claudius. Nero retaliated by trying to drown her, and when that failed, arranged to have her murdered by a centurion.

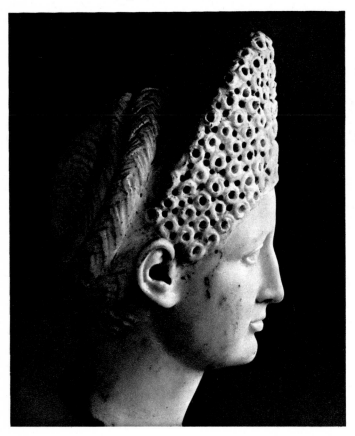

(*above*) This fantastic and extraordinary coiffure was popular in fashionable Rome at the end of the first century A.D. The tiara of false curls was several inches high.

(*left*) Poppaea, who was the second wife of Nero, died from a blow administered by her husband. This small alabaster head is another fine example of the stylised hair arrangement affected by Roman ladies of the period and shows how the natural hair was wound in a plait at the back of the head.

26

This very personal portrait of a young woman who lived in Egypt under the Roman Empire in the second century A.D., comes from her tomb at Fayoum. She has parted her hair in the centre with a chignon on top and wears the double pearl ear-rings and choker of beads which we shall see in many later portraits.

This idealized, almost academically formal picture from a fresco at Herculanaeum is called *The Writer*, and was at one time thought to be of Sappho. It shows a young girl with carefully dressed curls and a pretty face whose dreamy expression might be that of a nineteenth century portrait.

The Bikini in Sicily, 400 A.D.

In 1951 excavations near Piazza Armerina in Sicily brought to light the ruins of a luxurious villa and revealed a mosaic pavement in a remarkable state of preservation. On it were seen an astonishing series of pictures of girl gymnasts. The world was amazed to find that on the beaches of the Mediterranean fifteen hundred years ago the girls were dressed in exactly the same bikinis as they wear to-day. For the two-piece bathing suit was thought to be a new and rather vulgar modern fashion when it was launched several years before these fascinating mosaics were rediscovered. The Sicilian girls are shown with their hair curled but flying in the wind, their bodies almost naked but their eyes carefully made-up. To-day we lack only the victor's wreath, here being presented to the girl with the striped parasol: the brief loin-cloth and still briefer brassière are identical to those we are accustomed to call bikinis.

29

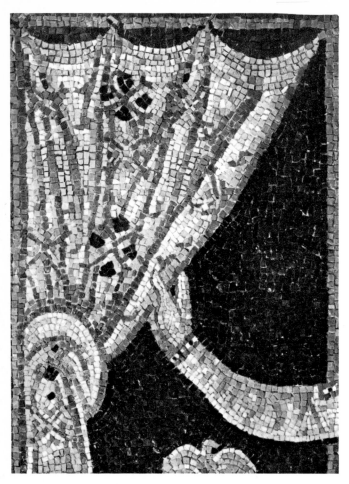

The Eclipse of the Nude

We seem to go indoors. The golden light of the classical sun has faded, the curtains are drawn against the dark and wintry atmosphere of the North, and the nude has vanished. The glitter of mosaic shows us hieratic figures painted to look like idols, smothered in elaborate robes and with the nimbus, not yet a wholly religious symbol, around their jewelled heads.

When we emerge after the long twilight of the dark ages, we are confronted with a totally different picture. Faces are no longer painted but pale, with small inconspicuous eyes; long fair hair falls straight onto the shoulders and slender bodies are elongated and flattened by stiff bodices. In the Gothic half-light magnificent tapestries show richly attired figures "with those white throats and tight bodices, those sparkling eyes resplendent with smiling beauty" sung by the Minnesingers, who praise the pale, proud ladies for whom the knights joust in the Courts of Love. Villon writes his poems to the "Dames du Temps Jadis", and the Romance of the Rose gives a new literary form to erotic imagination.

The love of magnificence and fantasy is illustrated in superb manuscripts: ladies in trailing gowns of brilliant colours and improbable hats talk to their gallants on flower-spangled meadows, or inhabit a world of the imagination surrealistic in its strangeness. The violence of medieval life is masked by courtly graces but behind a facade of beauty and chivalry the Dance of Death is ever present and the contrast between life and death, riches and poverty, tenderness and cruelty, has never been so acute.

The only known portrait of the Empress Galla Placidia, who after an adventurous life eventually ruled the Western Empire.

Church bells form an ever-clanging chorus to daily life and the mason's hammer can be heard all over Europe, for men are busy building the Gothic cathedrals which are amongst the most overwhelming tokens of man's potentiality for good. The influence of Christianity makes maternity one of the great themes and the Virgin with Child offers a new type of beauty; the happy young mother with her babe usurps the place of the naked goddesses of love and fertility. As the fourteenth century progresses the restrictions of decorative and symbolic art give way to natural portraiture and scattered throughout the churches of Europe are statues of astonishing liveliness. The blonde with curls makes her appearance and the gay little Virgin of Toulouse is ancestor to a long line of rosy beauties.

When the nude at last reappears a complete change of stance is evident. The sway-back, which comes and goes through the centuries, assumes grotesque proportions, and the medieval maiden is portrayed with protruding stomach, low-slung buttocks and small breasts placed high on her elongated torso.

31

(*above*) This Venetian Salome in St. Mark's is shown with long fair hair, waved and falling on her shoulders, her head bound with an elaborate jewelled fillet.

(*above*) Most Byzantine women, whether saints or court ladies, wore heavy make-up, long ear-rings and jewelled head-dresses topped by turbans.

(*left*) The golden robe of St. Agnes, one of the procession of virgins which decorates the great church of St. Apollinare Nuovo in Ravenna, is bordered with embroidery and reveals the skirt and sleeve of the dress beneath. The pattern of the jewelled yoke is repeated in the broad bracelet, a jewelled band encircles the chignon on her head and she carries a crown, the symbol of her martyrdom.

32

Byzantine
Magnificence

The opulence of the East shines in mosaic portraits

(*above*) This famous portrait of Theodora, the circus-driver who rose to be the wife of the Emperor Justinian, is in Ravenna. She is dressed in the purple robe of rank and wears a rich crown. Her face is heavily painted and her eyes exaggeratedly outlined in the Eastern manner.

(*left*) These portraits are thought to be of Antonina, wife of Belisarius, Justinian's great general and conqueror of Persians, Vandals and Ostrogoths, and their daughter Joanna. Their eyes and eye-brows, too, are strongly accentuated, their hair covers the ears and they wear magnificent bracelets and rings.

Fairy Tale Princesses

A slender figure of incomparable grace, richly clothed in court dress and wearing magnificent jewels: she represents *Taste* in the set of hangings known as *La Dame à la Licorne*, perhaps the richest in poetic invention of all Gothic tapestries.

This lady choosing jewels from her casket has the long, pale face, high forehead and narrow body with a flat bust so much admired in the opening years of the sixteenth century when this tapestry was woven, probably on the banks of the Loire.

3-

The Gothic world of wonder and imagination, glowing with colour and the glitter of many jewels

(*right*) St. Catherine is shown with a true fairy-tale princess's crown on her elaborately arranged hair, in Crivelli's *Crowning of the Virgin*.

(*above*) Two elegant ladies in fantastic hats and trailing gowns talk to their cavaliers in one of the magnificent calendar illustrations done for the Duc de Berry by the famous illuminator Pol de Limbourg.

(*right*) *Marcia engaged on a self-portrait*: this delightful French miniature of the fifteenth century shows an amateur artist at work. It is one of many illustrations in a book of the period dealing with famous women.

35

High Fantasy

(*left*) A startlingly surrealist illustration in a fifteenth century manuscript shows a woman transformed into a mermaid who blows a trumpet, but holds a violin.

(*below*) A gesture which will be repeated and painted down the ages is illustrated in this fourteenth century tapestry.

(*left*) The lightly veiled beauty who is offered the prize in this *Judgement of Paris* appears to be far advanced in pregnancy. Both she and her rival wear astonishing head-dresses and have the very large feet so often noticeable in Northern paintings.

36

The visit of Hippolyte, Queen of the Amazons, to Theseus, King of Athens, formed a fascinating subject for the imagination of Carpaccio. Here the Queen is seen accompanied by a group of her ladies.

The Sway Back

S-shaped figures, tiny breasts,
large stomachs and feet were admired
in the fifteenth century

(*above*) Ariadne is portrayed by an anonymous illustrator of
Ovid's *Heroides* as deserted on the monster-haunted shores of
Naxos, naked except for some remarkable shoes and a cap.

(*right*) An illustration from *Love's Game of Chess*, a splendid
manuscript executed for the instruction of the future King
Francis I of France, shows three Muses dancing round a tree.

The Charm of Love by the Master of Niederheim is a delightful example of the exaggeratedly long torso and small high breasts admired in the Middle Ages.

Natural Portraits in Stone

(left) Fragment of a French fifteenth century statuette.

A few unexpectedly lively portraits stand out among stylised effigies and give an intriguing glimpse of real women of the Middle Ages

(right) The pretty pouting face surrounded with curls belongs to a statue of the Virgin in Nôtre Dame of Toulouse. We have travelled a long way from the Eastern tradition of the Virgin enthroned to this enchanting but quite secular portrait. For this is obviously the face of a known and loved little person, not the personification of an idea. Symbolism has given place to the Western concept of individualism.

(*right*) Uta was the wife of one of the founders of the early thirteenth century cathedral at Naumberg in Saxony. In this extraordinarily lively portrait she holds the collar of her cloak up to her chin against the cold and has a vaguely amused expression.

(*above*) One of the treasures of Toledo Cathedral is this Virgin smiling at her Child who puts up his hand to caress her. The look of fond delight must have been taken from the expression of a real mother and bears no relation to the ikons of an earlier age.

(*right*) An astonishingly personal portrait is this statue from Lincoln Cathedral of Margaret of France, second wife of Edward I and sister of Philip the Fair. She appears to have inherited some of the good looks for which her brother was famed. She wears a crown and her curled hair is not entirely hidden by her veil.

41

Pale and Plucked

The bulging forehead, plucked to increase its apparent height,
the hair entirely hidden by huge hats and, as Chaucer said of Alisoun,
the carpenter's wife, the eyebrows plucked "full small"

The plucked bare forehead of her period cannot disguise the sulky good looks of this young girl painted by Petrus Christus. She is said to have been an Englishwoman, first the wife of Edward Grimston, and later Lady Talbot, though there is little evidence for this supposition. The stiffened velvet loop in front of her high drum-shaped hat is to prevent it sliding off.

A stiff translucent linen coif folded over a dome-shaped cap, covers the high forehead of this young Flemish woman and contrasts with the pale but glowing colour of her face. She was painted by Rogier van der Weyden, but as so often we are tantalised by knowing nothing of her history. Note the upslant of her large heavy-lidded eyes so typical of her period.

(*above*) This clear serene profile, known as the Princess of Trebizond, by Pisanello, is an extreme example of the fashion for high foreheads. The Princess wears a western version of the Turkish turban, swollen to huge dimensions, which reveals her large ears and barely balances on her bulging forehead.

(*right*) The long slender body, low waistline and slightly distended stomach admired at the time are exquisitely illustrated by Memling in this picture of Bathsheba stepping from her bath. Both she and her attendant wear folded coifs: even in the intimacy of the bedroom the hair is entirely hidden according to the dictates of fifteenth century fashion.

43

The New Beauty

The Renaissance preferred the angular grace and springy lines of youth to the ripeness of maturity. The nude re-appears, young and undeveloped. The faces are young, modest and gay, the hair yellow. Blondes are the acknow-ledged beauties and hair enormously important. Sometimes it flows free but more often it is plaited, twined and curled in imaginative ways and the forehead is left bare, though often decorated with jewels or softened by veils. The waist is not accentuated but the shoulders are broadened by voluminous puffed and slashed sleeves, the bosom is covered, and strong, slender necks are encircled with magnificent jewels – the string of pearls is not yet *de rigueur*.

The Church is still the main patron of art and the ladies of the time are often portrayed as madonnas, their demure expressions due more to downcast eyelids than religious preoccupations; and not until Victorian days will modesty and lowered lids again be considered important adjuncts to beauty.

The re-discovery of the classics set alight a perfect passion for language and learning and the treasures of Greek and Latin literature became available to the

44

whole reading public. For the first time many women were highly educated and often learned to speak several languages, the scandalous *Tale of Two Lovers*, the first real novelette to appear in Europe, which later became an embarrassment to its author when he was elected Pope, was read with delight, and Boccaccio's *Decameron* whiled away the time while the courtiers idled and the plague raged. It is an age of tremendous vigour when vast fortunes are made, huge palaces are built, great art collections and fine libraries are formed, but when beauty also is worshipped. Lorenzo the Magnificent himself wrote an ode in honour of Simonetta Vespucci the fabulous beauty who inspired a whole generation of artists. When she died her body was carried through the streets of Florence with her face uncovered so that all could see her loveliness, and Boccaccio on looking at the heavens, cried "her soul hath passed into the new star".

Young and Slender

(*above*) Botticelli's Venus rising from the sea is said to be a likeness of the famous beauty Simonetta Vespucci. The whole concept looks back with delight to the classic world it glorifies and is completely at variance with the Medieval spirit.

(*right*) This young woman's portrait is now to be seen on Italian banknotes. Her hair is curled, adorned with plaits and pearls which encircle the pony-tail, and topped with a feather.

*This vision of youth in fluttering veils,
flower-crowned, re-creates the long-forgotten beauties
of an unselfconscious pagan world.
Botticelli's lovely girls with flowing hair and perfect
proportions are like a breath of fresh air let into
the medieval world: their gentle serious faces and
slender bodies represent a new approach to beauty,
untouched by prudery.*

(*above*) Botticelli's *Primavera* was inspired by a poem on classical subjects by Poliziano, favourite poet and friend of Lorenzo the Magnificent. It re-opens a vista long closed, where beauty can flaunt itself unfettered by false modesty.

(*left*) The head of Flora in the *Primavera* is thought to be another portrait of Simonetta, whose beauty was the delight of Florentine artists and who was painted so often by Botticelli.

47

Renaissance Blondes

These two fifteenth century Siennese girls, painted by Neroccio de' Landi, have pensive dark eyes and classic features, but their chief attraction is their long fair hair, bleached, curled and hanging loose, but with a veil or jewelled cap partly covering it. The full length of Claudia Quinta is notable for the slender perfection of her hands and her feet shod in jewelled sandals.

A contemporary said of Lucrezia Borgia, here shown as Flora by Bartolommeo Veneziano, " Her hair is a bright gold and her eyes blue, her neck white and slender. She is very beautiful but her charm of manner is still more striking". Her small bosom would have been envied in the 1920's.

The Fetish of Hair

Every now and again the immemorial fascination of hair becomes an obsession. The Victorian counterparts of these fifteenth century curiosities can be seen on pp. 136-7. The Magdalen above is dressed solely in her rippling locks which reach her ankles, while the painted wooden Eve on the left depends somewhat less successfully on her hair for raiment.

Simonetta Vespucci came to Florence when very young and attracted the attention of Giuliano de' Medici, brother of Lorenzo the Magnificent. The poet Poliziano describes "the winding ringlets of her golden head" and Pollaiuolo, who painted this portrait of her as Cleopatra, considered her a symbol of beauty. She died of consumption when she was twenty-three.

Quattrocento Coiffures

Women of the late fifteenth century, not yet the slaves of professional hair-dressers, displayed immense ingenuity in arranging their hair, often bleaching it and adding many false plaits.

52

Two of the luxurious courtesans for whom Venice was famous are painted by Carpaccio sitting on the terrace of their house. Their hair is bleached, frizzed and topped with false chignons, and they wear large necklaces and dresses with elaborately slashed and tied sleeves.

The Lowered Lid

The demure expression of many Madonnas owes more to their lowered eyes than religious vocation. Parmigiano's *Virgin with the Long Neck (left)* has an almost worldly air about her curled and jewelled coiffure. A long neck has always been admired: for a prospective sixteenth century sister-in-law wrote to her brother of his as yet unseen bride that "if her neck were two finger breadths longer she would be quite a beauty". Perhaps Luini *(below, left)* best expresses real saintliness though Raphael's *Madonna of the Goldfinch (below, right)* has become the archetype of the pure and holy, accepted throughout the world as a vision of the ideal virgin.

The Candid Eye

These composed and dignified portraits of worldly young women (amongst the first society portraits known to us) are far from the angularities of the previous century and represent a new outlook on the human body. The profile by Piero della Francesca (*right*) is unexpectedly modern and the head by Ghirlandaio (*right, below*) has a very forthright expression, despite the fantasy of the curiously curled front hair. A variant of this coiffure is seen in another contemporary portrait (*below, left*) in which a coral necklace encircles the sitter's strong neck, and a matching ornament holds back her long straight hair while another buttons on a delicate lawn over-bodice.

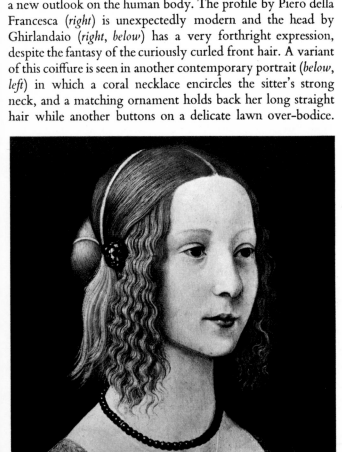

In a cold climate

In England and the Low Countries the type of woman admired was different from her Italian contemporary. Portraits show women bedecked like idols, reminiscent of Byzantine beauties of a thousand or more years before. Smothered in fabulous jewels, their figures are obscured by skirts rigid with embroidery and by boned bodices which flatten and deform them. Only the face and hands are visible; the hands angular and stiffly jointed, the face divorced from the body and merely a focal point for elaborate brocades and ruffs. For a time the hair and ears are hidden by architectural head-dresses and the eyes are the predominant feature, despite the fact that they are devoid of artifice and no lines outline or enlarge them. Later portraits show the severe Tudor coifs discarded in favour of immense lace ruffs which frame heavily painted faces surmounted by hair which "was of force curled, frizzed and crisped". The moral code was as rigid as the stiff dresses, yet in spite of these restrictions women were by no means as repressed as might be expected. At that time a widow automatically became a member of her husband's guild and could carry on his trade, and in London there was a women's silk guild.

The names of the materials they wore are poems in themselves — bays, says and sarcenets were English, but perpetuanas, mackadoes and frizadoes were Flemish, and the women portrayed in the following pages are dressed in the then popular colours of sops-in-wine, popinjay-green and sand-marigold.

The Age of Chivalry was over but the love of pageantry persisted and the famous Field of the Cloth of Gold was an exhibition of splendour such as was loved by Henry VIII, and later by Elizabeth.

It was an age of adventure, when the discovery of the Northwest passage fired the imagination of the populace and Raleigh named a great area of land in a New World after his young Queen. It is a period more easily apprehended by sound than sight, Shakespeare has made its language and thoughts familiar to us, but it is difficult to associate these women, barely able to move in their jewelled and embroidered dresses, with the actions of daily life.

Only in the paintings of the mysterious School of Fontainebleau does humanity break through the heraldic trappings. In this enchanting world alone women appear stripped of their cumbrous garments, their nudity cunningly veiled, and the breast reappears as a symbol of love.

Eyes but no Ears

At the Court of Henry VIII severe coifs of architectural inspiration entirely cover head and ears

(*above*) Ann Boleyn was credited with long black hair and slanting dark eyes but this portrait by Holbein allows only the latter to be seen. She was maid of honour to Queen Catherine when she attracted the King, and after his separation from Catherine was secretly married to him. She bore him a daughter, Elizabeth, and then, having most unwisely incurred his jealousy was beheaded only three years later.

(*right*) Ann Cresacre married John, the only son of Sir Thomas More, the great Lord Chancellor. This drawing, a study for Holbein's painting of the More family, shows her in the flat-chested Tudor dress with protruding stomach which, unlike most fashions, has never returned to favour.

58

Elizabeth of Austria, Queen of France, is shown by Clouet wearing a close-fitting ruff, her hair parted in the centre, and drawn back from the forehead over two rolls. She wears a cap of pearls and jewels and immense stones are sewn onto the yoke of her brocade gown and puffed sleeves.

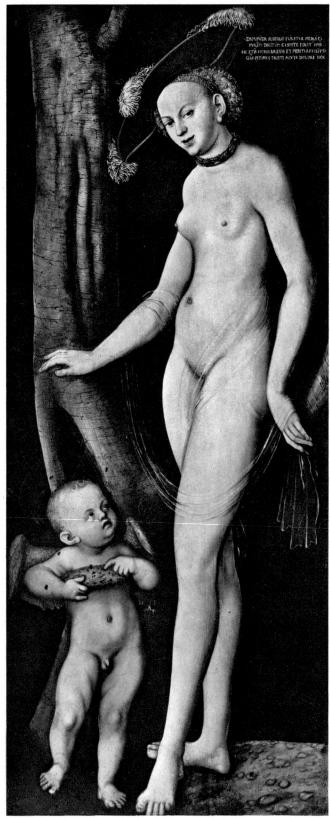

DVM PVER ALVEOLO FVRATVR MELLA CVPIDO
FVRANTI DIGITVM CVSPIDE FIXIT APIS
SIC ETIA NOBIS BREVIS ET PERITVRA VOLVPTAS
QVA PETIMVS TRISTI MIXTA DOLORE NOCET

The Elongated Line

The exaggeratedly long body and high small breasts of the previous century are now modified into a slender figure. The S-shaped body is straightened, the long torso remains, but is now balanced by proportionally long legs and a bosom of normal size.

(*left*) High rounded breasts and extremely long legs give elegance to these two nudes painted by Cranach. He has endowed Eve (*extreme left*) with much charm. Venus (*left*) is shown naked save for a superb necklace and an elaborate feather-trimmed hat perched on a jewel-studded net which completely hides her hair. Note that the ears and feet are remarkably large, for their smallness is not yet considered to be a criterion of beauty.

(*right*) The exaggerated slimness of Englebrecht's elegant Saint Helena is accentuated by her pointed velvet basque and by the long draperies which fall from her slender hands. Everything about her is consciously elongated. It will be four hundred years before height and extreme slenderness are once again accounted beautiful by the pre-Raphaelites.

61

A Frame
for the Face

Elaborate lace ruffs form
a decorative background to painted
faces and a plethora of pearls

(*right*) A hitherto unpublished portrait of the Virgin Queen
shows her painted in translucent tones which give her the
porcelain pink and white complexion so much admired.

(*above*) Rubens delighted to paint Brigitta Spinola, the
daughter of a Genoese General, and here shows her with an
immense millstone ruff which completely divorces her plump
face and tightly curled hair from her body.

(*right*) Princess Isabella of Savoy is painted by Pourbus
wearing an open ruff of stiffened lace, her hair arranged over a
high frame decorated with frizzed locks, jewels and ribbons.

Mary Fitton, a celebrated Elizabethan beauty, was the mistress of the Earl of Pembroke. She was a maid of honour to the Queen and is identified by some as the Dark Lady of Shakespeare's sonnets. Her magnificent costume and jewellery are outstanding even in an age of unparalleled ostentation.

The Round Bosom

(*right*) *Peace*, an exquisite example of the lovely nudes which were a speciality of the painters of the Fontainebleau School.

(*below*) The Virgin, by Fouquet (*below, right*) has long been known to be a portrait of Agnes Sorel, and if ever there had been any doubt it would be dispelled by the juxtaposition of this acknowledged but anonymous portrait of the famous mistress of Charles VII (*below, left*). She was a maid of honour at the Court and became the mother of four daughters by the King, one of whom was Jeanne de Valois. She died mysteriously and Charles' son Louis XI, was thought by some to have been her poisoner although there was no proof.

In his famous *Allegory of Time and Love* Bronzino originally gave Venus only a tiara of pearls—the drapery was probably added in a more prudish age. This splendid nude was sent as a gift from Cosimo, Grand Duke of Florence, to Francis I, King of France.

The Enigmatic Mistresses of Fontainebleau

These gay naked and half-naked ladies are a complete contrast to their richly apparelled but severe contemporaries in England.

Only the finest veils shadow their nudity but even in the bath they wear their tear-drop pearl ear-rings.

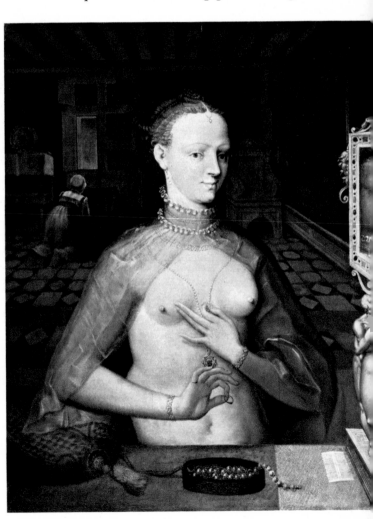

Among the many supposed likenesses of Diane de Poitiers, the famous mistress of Henry II of France, are these two portraits. (*above*) She is seen in the guise of Sabina Poppaea, wife of Nero, and (*right*) at her toilette clad in nothing more than a ruff and veil of fine gauze. Although ten years older than Henry she inspired him with a deep love when he was Dauphin and he loved her until his death. When he came to the throne she was virtual queen, while his wife Catherine de' Medici lived in comparative obscurity. As Henry was a most generous lover Diane became enormously rich, but after his death the Queen insisted on her returning the crown jewels, and exchanging her enchanting water-side chateau of Chenonceaux for the vast and turreted grandeur of Chambord.

This famous picture shows Gabrielle d'Estrées, the mistress of Henry IV of France, and her sister in the bath. It hung for many years in the Préfecture de Police in Paris, where nineteenth century prudery hid it beneath a curtain. One day it was found to be missing and for many years it was lost, which may perhaps account for the number of copies which exist. Gabrielle was descended from an ancient family of France and is the best known among the favourites of the genial Gascon King, to whom she bore several children.

Veiled Nudity

(*left*) La Ricolina, one of the beauties of the French Court, displays the favourite Fontainebleau combination of nudity, veils and jewels. Note the large ears on this otherwise delicate head and her very high breasts. (*below*) A lightly veiled beauty with the full round breasts and well developed thighs characteristic of this period, hesitates between the choice of a handsomely-dressed young lover and a rich but elderly suitor.

In a mysterious garden a group of women sit or stand around a bathing pool, naked, or wearing only veils and fantastic garden hats of immense size, similar to those worn to-day in the Midi. The exaggerated length of leg alone links them with the nudes, so different in spirit, which Cranach was painting across the Rhine, and their full round breasts are typical of the Fontainebleau beauties. In the distance we see a gateway with a classical pediment and on the far horizon the towers of a fabulous city.

The Golden Age

At no period has a passionate cult of beauty for its own sake been more triumphantly proclaimed than when the great Venetian painters were in their prime. Titian's and Tintoretto's superb portraits of large-limbed women, their golden tresses intertwined with jewels, successfully fuse the ideal with the real. It is the beauty of slow movement, full breasts and vast riches. The luxury of Venice, perhaps the most extreme ever known in Europe, was used to enhance, not obscure their beauty. Jewels high light white flesh and corn-yellow hair, magnificent velvets and embroideries provide a frame for splendid shoulders, but are readily discarded to display the firm naked bodies beneath.

Hair was enormously admired and never hidden beneath coifs or powdered as in previous and subsequent generations, but shown proudly, elaborately plaited, decorated with pearls, or brushed out its full length for all to admire. No pains were spared to acquire the colour and glint of gold, and hair was often bleached

70

by wearing a broad brimmed but crownless straw hat to expose it more thoroughly to sunlight. It was usually worn drawn back to reveal both forehead and ears which, after the first years of the sixteenth century, were hung with ear-rings. For the next three hundred years tear-drop pearls were the ear-rings chosen by the majority of women. Breasts were often bare and rouged and *"espoitrinement à la Venise"* became notorious. The extravagance became such that laws were passed prohibiting certain luxuries. The Doge's daughters alone were exempt from these restrictions, and on one occasion a niece of the Doge was sent home to change her attire because, in contravention to the law, her whole dress was of cloth of gold, whereas only sleeves were allowed to be made of gold or silver. But the regulations were powerless to check the myriad refinements of luxury and the Venetian women continued to adorn themselves with every form of magnificence regardless of the sumptuary laws.

Venetian Beauties

Sensuous large-limbed figures
painted in sumptuous colours

(*above*) From the calmness of expression of this head, a detail
of Salome by Titian, one would never imagine she was holding the head of John the Baptist on a platter. Her eyebrows
each describe a perfect arc, repeated by the line of her hair,
which is parted in the centre and falls in long curled tresses.

(*right*) The magnificent flesh and solid body of this Venus by
Titian is richer in form than that of the Quattrocento girls:
here the maturity of full summer is preferred to the promise
of youth extolled in the previous century. The lips are full,
the hair yellow like ripe corn, the breasts large and ample.

Tintoretto's splendid illustration of the time-honoured story of Leda and the swan shows a nude with the full and rounded perfection in which the sixteenth century delighted and the Venetian masters excelled.

73

Splendid Trappings

Magnificent brocades and velvets, shining satins and embroideries, pearls, precious stones and furs adorn these handsome women of the Renaissance, who wind jewels in their hair and hang pearls from their ears.

(*above*) There were many laws in Venice prohibiting certain luxuries and some furs were on the forbidden list, but marten was permitted as we see in this portrait of Anthea by Parmigiano. She holds the head of her marten tie in her gloved hand and like most women of her day, she wears ear-rings of drop pearls and puts a third at the parting of her hair.

(*right*) The enormous dark eyes, strong eyebrows and firm features of this lovely but nameless Spanish girl, painted by El Greco, are framed by a veil and magnificent fur collar.

(*right*) The wife of one of Florence's leading citizens, Lucrezia Panciatichi, was painted by Bronzino wearing a dress with puffed and shirred satin sleeves which emphasise the beauty of her hands. She wears a necklace of pearls and chains of jewels decorate her hair which is wound round her head.

(*above*) Daughter of an illustrious Venetian family, Caterina Cornaro married a de Lusignan and was the Queen of Cyprus when Titian painted this portrait, though it is doubtful whether she ever sat for him. At the death of her husband the Republic insisted Cyprus should be ceded to Venice, but in return gave her lands at Asolo, where her castle still stands.

(*right*) Cecilia, Titian's wife, is thought to have posed for *La Bella* and perhaps for his Venus of Urbino. The rich blue dress with its puffed sleeves reveals her fine neck and shoulders and its splendour is rivalled by her bleached and jewelled hair.

75

Opulent Charms

*Sensuous beauty at its best is portrayed in these
paintings of Venetian women where
the flesh tones of their full and voluptuous bodies
contrast with the richness of their golden hair
and glittering jewels.*

(*above*) Pharaoh's daughter is depicted by Veronese looking
down on Moses in the basket. She and her attendants wear
romantic robes and draperies and jewelled ornaments of great
richness and variety in their fair hair, which is wound around
their heads and arranged in short curls on their foreheads.

(*left*) The model for this Salome was Titian's daughter,
Lavinia Vecelli, "the person dearest to him in all the world".
She wears the drop pearl ear-ring adopted by most women of
her day, a brocade dress with gauze draperies around the
shoulders which fall back to reveal her strong young arms,
and on her golden hair, threaded with pearls, a jewelled tiara.

76

The calm sensuousness and glorious colour of Susannah's ample body is enriched by the jewelled accessories of her toilette and the multitude of intricate golden plaits with which Tintoretto has adorned her.

One of the best known and most perfect of all naked portraits, timeless in its perfection, is Titian's Venus of Urbino. There are several somewhat similar versions but in this one she is seen with her little brown and white dog curled up asleep at the end of her bed, while in the background her maids get out her clothes from a huge carved and gilded *cassone*.

Laura Dianti, a beautiful bourgeoise of Ferrara, became the mistress of the Duke Alfonso d'Este after the death of his wife, who was none other than the famous Lucrezia Borgia, daughter of Pope Alexander VI, about whose relationships many strange stories are told. There exists a similar picture of the lovers, also by Titian, in which Laura is seen fully dressed.

The Saturated Curve

Rubens was fifty-three when he married Helena Fourment the daughter of his dead wife's sister, then aged sixteen. He delighted in painting his young wife and among his many portraits few are more attractive than the one in which her rosy flesh is bulging out of an incongruous fur wrap, her fair curls hanging round her shoulders. Another, equally appealing, shows her in a tightly corseted velvet dress, a fine handkerchief over her shoulders and a velvet cap trimmed with a huge feather perched on her head.

Few of the women immortalised by the Venetian masters are known to us by name, but in a later generation it is the young wives of the two great painters shown on these pages who symbolise the lush beauty of their day. We know that Rembrandt was only twenty-four when he married the lovely Saskia van Uylenborch, then twenty-two. He painted her many times with great love and understanding and she was the model for this well-covered but beguiling Bathsheba.

Sense & Sensuality

The lingering influence of the High Renaissance is still noticeable in the luscious charms of the Restoration court ladies and a double chin appears to be as much admired as a fine décolletage. Bosoms are largely exposed and the *déshabillés* such that ladies go to morning service "half-dressed, like angels", and many of them are painted with their robes arranged to reveal voluptuous charms.

Eyes are large and protrude slightly beneath heavy lids. Complexions of wax-work perfection are achieved by much paint and powder, sometimes accentuated by patches. Ears are still emphasised by drop pearl ear-rings, and a contemporary poet says that for every woman "Must need be had – two Pearl Pears, Pearl necklace, large and Oriental". Pearls are the fashionable jewel and a large string worn around the base of the throat essential to every beauty and the first gift of a successful lover. It is fascinating to note how ubiquitous and how long lasting was this fashion – indeed, the pearl choker is still seen to-day

Hair is worn its natural colour and no longer braided and piled on top. The head is massed with close curls or hung with hook-shaped ringlets, the back hair twisted in a small flat bun. Soon follows one of the recurrent periods when no hair is visible. Caps and lappets frame the face, but curls are banned. With the end of the seventeenth century opulence diminishes, neat waists return and boned bodices, laced up the front, constrict and flatten the breasts, until Fielding speaks of "slender young women, who seem rather intended to hang up in the hall of an anatomist than for any other purpose", and says that "no woman can be genteel who is not flat before". As the bosom becomes less important more attention is paid to the extremities, hands and arms are set off by wide sleeves and frills of lace, neatly shod feet peep out from beneath skirts which are now short enough to reveal them. Some of these satin clad ladies affect a modest demeanour, but all look worldly and sensual. They lead sheltered indoor lives in which nature plays no part. They drink chocolate, a new beverage which has become the rage, served by negro pages or perhaps by dwarfs, who are still imported from Spain and Sicily. They play cribbage or read the *Lives of the Rakes* while small brown and white spaniels lie at their feet.

It is the fashion to write diaries and John Evelyn's is a mine of information

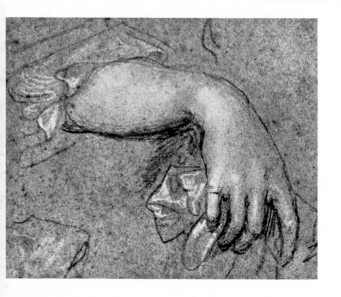

about the happenings of everyday life. The Comte de Gramont, married to La Belle Hamilton, recounts the amorous scandals of Charles II's court. Madame de Sevigné writes her famous letters. And Pepys in his delightful and human pages tells us such details as "my wife this day (1669) put on first her French gown, called a Sac".

Curls and Pearls

Heavy eyelids and ample bosoms, together with the inevitable pearls, were essential adjuncts to beauty when the two Charles's were on the throne of England

(*above*) Frances, later Duchess of Lennox and Richmond, often called "La Belle Stuart", refused Charles II her favours until after her marriage, when the King gave her the famous dressing-table set known as the Lennoxlove silver, which sold recently for £10,000. She was a tom-boy and very merry, "with her sweet eye, little Roman nose and excellent *taille*" and was known for her taste in clothes, though it was said that no one had more beauty and less wit. Charles ordered Roettiers to make an engraving of her as Britannia and stamp her portrait, complete with trident and helmet, to watch over the coinage of his realm—which she still does today.

(*right*) Elizabeth Hamilton married the Comte de Gramont, who came to England at the time of the Restoration. Her brother, Anthony, was the author of the *Mémoires du Comte de Gramont*, an amusing and frivolous account of the courts of France and England during the late seventeenth century. She wears the inevitable drop pearl ear-rings and corkscrew curls.

(*below*) Venetia, Lady Digby whose beauty formed the theme of Ben Jonson's *Eupheme* was the wife of Sir Kenelm Digby. Lord Clarendon said she was a "lady of extreme beauty as well as of extraordinary fame" and rumour was constantly busy with her reputation. She was found dead in her bed and a miniature by Peter Oliver of her on her death-bed still exists. This portrait by Van Dyck, complete with mythological trappings and cupids, shows her with the ringlets, pearls and double chin required by the taste of the seventeenth century.

(*above*) Frances Howard, Duchess of Richmond, was celebrated for her vanity as well as her beauty and it is plain to see that she was proud of her pearl-hung blonde curls, her splendid bosom, and her white skin here set off by black velvet and white lawn. She was married three times and one of her suitors, William Seymour, Earl of Hertford, killed himself when he was rejected.

(*above*) Barbara Villiers, Countess of Castlemaine, later Duchess of Cleveland, was a dark-haired beauty of imperious temperament and Charles's mistress for nearly twelve years. Her son by the King became Duke of Grafton and the ancestor of the lines of Hertford and Castlereagh. Her daughter married the Earl of Lichfield and became ancestor of Lord Melbourne and Sir Anthony Eden. In all, twelve prime ministers have been descended from her, and the present Queen numbers a Villiers among her forebears. This unfinished miniature by Samuel Cooper is said to be the best likeness ever made of her.

(*above*) Louise de Kerouaille, Duchess of Portsmouth, came to England in the train of "Minette", Charles II's beloved sister, and on the latter's death was sent to console him for her loss. Evelyn, the diarist, speaks of her "baby face", but she was always very unpopular, partly because she was known to advance the French cause, but also because she managed to extract vast sums of money from the easy-going Charles. Her son by him became Duke of Richmond.

(*right*) Hortense Mancini, Duchess of Mazarin, was one of the "Mazarinettes" brought to Paris by their uncle, Cardinal Mazarin, to make important marriages and consolidate his position. After an adventurous life she came to London and became a favourite of Charles II who gave her a pension.

Nell Gwyn, the orange seller from Drury Lane theatre who became one of Charles's favourite companions and a rival to the Duchess of Portsmouth, was painted naked for him by Lely. And the portrait is said to have been hidden at times behind another picture. She bears a strong resemblance to her rival, the Duchess of Cleveland (*see above left*). Whether there has been some confusion in crediting the picture, or whether Charles's taste was as definite as it appears to be, cannot be known for certain, but contemporaries were agreed that Nell was "a mighty pretty creature".

87

The Round
and
Dimpled Face

These two portraits by Mignard are both of Louise de la Vallière, the famous mistress of Louis XIV. She was a golden haired girl from Tours who came to the court as lady-in-waiting to the Duchess of Orleans. The King fell deeply in love with her and she returned his feelings with real sincerity. Their liaison became officially recognised, but the young Duchess was extremely pious and never forgave herself for what she considered a grave fault and when only twenty-six she entered a convent. After a time the King induced her to return to the world and for a brief period she emerged from her seclusion and resumed her relationship with him. Later however she was supplanted in his favour by Madame de Montespan and, heartbroken, she took the veil in a Carmelite Order and under the name of Marie-Louise de la Misericorde lived for thirty-four years in the absolute quiet of a nunnery, wearing the white habit of the Order. In Mignard's portraits her dimpled face and rosebud mouth remain seductive even when her curls are hidden by a coif.

In the reigns of Louis XIV and XV
a softly feminine but worldly beauty
was the French ideal and a pouting
mouth and plump figure characterise
the royal mistresses

(*above*) The Duchesse de Chateauroux was one of three sisters
who became Louis xv's mistresses but the first to acquire
notoriety, for it was she who persuaded him to take a personal
part in the war against Austria. She accompanied him on his
expedition to Flanders but when he fell ill the King's great
fear of hell caused him to dismiss his mistress and promise
to live a reformed life. For a time they were reconciled but
not long afterwards the Duchess died suddenly, and Louis said
of her that she was the only woman he had really loved.

(*left*) A typical example of the plump and pretty little women
admired at the French court is the *Lady at her toilet* by Watteau.

The Small Sophisticated Head

For a brief moment women allowed their simply dressed hair to reveal the natural shape of their heads

(*above*) When the Venetian pastellist Rosalba Carriera visited Paris in 1720 she painted this portrait of an unknown lady at the court of the Regent. A triple row of pearls to accentuate the long neck appears for the first, but not the last, time.

(*right*) The Comtesse de Vintimille, here painted by Nattier as Flora, was one of three sisters, who all became mistresses of King Louis xv. She died in child-birth and her son was so very like his father that he was nicknamed the "Demi-Louis".

90

(*above*) The small neat head of Marie Françoise de Pedrigeon is covered with a satin drapery which matches the crisp folds of her skirt, set into a pointed, very trim little waist. An embroidered shoe appears beneath her skirts, and only one row of pearls encircles her plump neck.

(*above*) Allan Ramsay's *Painter's Wife* sets off her small neat features and head by a lace cape and a chignon of flowers.
(*above right*) Catherine, daughter of Henry Hyde, Earl of Clarendon and Rochester, married the Duke of Queensberry when very young. She was a friend and patroness of the poets John Gay and Matthew Prior and called by Walpole "Prior's Kitty, ever young". Jervas executed this portrait of the Duchess, arrayed in the severe manner of the time. Her hair is entirely covered by a cap whose lappets hide her ears; but her large eyes and clear features give an indication of the beauty for which she was famed.

(*right*) This portrait by the Swiss pastellist Liotard of his young niece, Mademoiselle Lavergne, is usually called *The Beautiful Reader*. He shows her with a boned and laced bodice to flatten her bust, similar to that worn by *La Belle Bourgeoise* opposite but, as an unmarried girl, she wears a cross on a thin black cord instead of the pearl necklace of the married woman.

92

The Sheltered Life

Curls disappear and the hair is brushed back and sometimes
entirely hidden beneath caps or hats

The opulent charms of Largillière's *La Belle Bourgeoise* are set off by fine lace, large pearls
and a hat which her husband probably found as ridiculous as she thought it becoming.

Elaborate costumes and fanciful head dresses frame small faces from which th hair is drawn back severely to expose th

(*above*) Lady Mary Wortley Montagu, the eldest daughter of Evelyn, Earl of Kingstone, was widely known for her spite, brilliant wit and beauty. Her friendship and quarrel with Pope and her equivocal life made her much discussed in her life-time, but she achieved lasting fame through her *Letters from Constantinople* written when her husband was Ambassador at the Porte. She loved exotic and eccentric clothes and is pictured here by Jonathan Richardson in Turkish robes.

(*right*) Maria, Countess of Coventry, one of the two lovely Gunning sisters, also wears Turkish dress in this portrait by Liotard. He had spent some years in the Near East and was known to his intimates as "The Turk" and loved to make his sitters wear Oriental dress in memory of his travels.

94

nd Frills

orehead. Tight bodices and sleeves define
he body and upper arms but draperies
r flounces reveal wrists and pale hands

(*above*) This charming and elegant picture by Fragonard, known as *Le Billet Doux*, is probably a portrait of the artist's wife.

(*left*) Elizabeth Gunning, Duchess of Hamilton and later Duchess of Argyll, was the sister of the Countess of Coventry. She took England, and indeed Europe, by storm with her beauty, which was only equalled by her kindness of heart. She went south for her health and in Naples became the intimate friend of Emma Hamilton before her marriage to Sir William, and countenanced her in public when most English ladies were at best coldly civil. Her influence helped to make Emma accepted in society and her early death, which the southern sun had proved powerless to prevent, was a sorrow to all who had known this lovely young woman.

The Encircled Neck

Consummate taste transforms a swirl of silk and lace into distinguished elegance: no hair softens the brow but pearls or a ribbon decorate the neck.

(*above*) Mary, Countess Howe, here portrayed in all her superb finery by Gainsborough, married Richard Howe, who was commander-in-chief in the Channel at the battle of "The Glorious First of June". For this famous victory he was made Admiral of the Fleet and created Earl Howe.

(*right*) Kitty Fisher, one of the most celebrated and intelligent courtesans of her day, was the original of Kitty Willis in *The Belle's Stratagem*. Reynolds painted this portrait at about the time of her marriage to Mr. Norris, shortly after which she died, somewhat mysteriously, "a victim of cosmetics".

96

The Beguiling Look

The eyes alone speak: dark and shining,
they are neither artificially enlarged
nor outlined, only their natural brilliance
is allowed to enchant.

(*above*) This mysterious picture of a Cistercian or Carthusian Sister standing in a wild and romantic landscape, looking proudly out of her well-draped and worldly robes, was painted by Jean Barbault, who worked and died in Rome in the middle of the eighteenth century.

(*left*) Mademoiselle Fel, an opera singer, met the painter La Tour when she was only twenty-one and remained his friend until his death. He drew her in the head-dress of blue gauze trimmed with gold braid in which she played Amelite when Rameau's opera *Zoroastre* was produced in 1749.

Art and Artifice

The women of the eighteenth century are petite and pouting, corseted and coiffed – the opulent nudes of the previous century have vanished. The small face, the short nose, the round chin are admired. The bosom is no longer exposed but framed in frills and laces, feet are revealed in exquisite shoes trimmed with jewelled buckles, necks and wrists accentuated by ties of flowers and ribbons instead of pearls, and the delights of "les dessous" become a favourite theme. Sometimes the elaboration of the dresses and their trimmings all but overwhelms the beauty of the wearers, but the rosy nudity beneath is never quite forgotten and Boucher and Fragonard record with exquisite felicity the plump and pretty women of their day.

Never was coquetry carried to such extremes. Everything was made for the delight of feminine taste, not only extravagant furbelows but porcelain, furniture and decorations, for this is a boudoir world, silken-soft and heavy with scent. The satins and taffetas woven under Royal patronage are in colours chosen

98

by the King's favourites – Nattier blue and rose du Barry have passed into the language – and the name of the Pompadour has become synonymous with the most exquisite artificiality the world has ever known.

The vast palaces of Versailles and Marly grew ever larger and only the splash of fountains enlivened the long vistas of ordered gardens, from which any riot of flowers was carefully excluded. As a contrast to the cold magnificence of court etiquette, the small painted boudoir was devised and soon Marie Antoinette was to create her Petit Trianon in order to sample the delights of the simple life. Meanwhile flowers are merely an accessory to a toilette, children nothing more than cupids, nature at best a backcloth for a *Fête Champêtre* and mythology only an excuse for further licence in portraiture and poetry.

In England silks are rivalled by fine muslins and snow-white fichus, and coloured ribbon sashes set off the modest décolletage, powdered hair and dark sparkling eyes of the great ladies. It is a fashion that will have enduring influence for it coincides with the great period of portrait painting in this country. The superb records left

by Reynolds, Gainsborough and Romney have become part of our heritage and the beauties of this era are still the most admired. But as the storm of the French Revolution approaches, the winds of reason ruffle the carefully coiffed heads of the ladies of the *ancien régime*. Women are now portrayed out-of-doors, their hair no longer powdered and with long locks blowing round their shoulders. The age of artifice is over.

Baroque Bravura

Reticence is cast to the winds and
saints are dressed as if on their way to a ball
and virtues as if they were court ladies

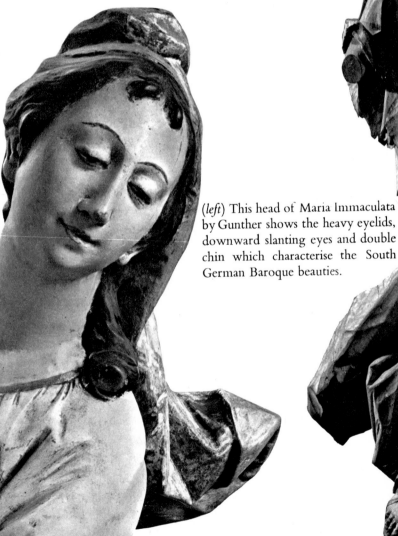

(*left*) This head of Maria Immaculata
by Gunther shows the heavy eyelids,
downward slanting eyes and double
chin which characterise the South
German Baroque beauties.

(*above*) The elaborate draperies of this
angel's robe appear to float in the air
and illustrate well the contemporary
feeling for movement. Note her protuberant and drooping eyelids.

A superb example of the love of splendour is Fortitudo, one of the masterpieces of the Corsican sculptor, Serpotta, who shows the Virtue with a magnificent feathered head-dress.

St. Kunigund in her splendid white and gold robes looks more like a queen dressed for a court ceremony than a saint. She wears a golden crown and gold ear-rings and necklace.

Rosy Perfection

Pink and blue silks and satins,
ribbons and flowers are used to enhance
the rosy nudity beneath

(*left*) Among Boucher's many portraits of women none is more enchanting than this one of the young Madame Bergeret in her lovely satin dress standing in an idealised garden. Around her neck, instead of the hitherto ubiquitous pearls, she wears frilled lace tied with a bow; on her shoulder and her smooth small head are bouquets of flowers; while from one hand dangles a flat, flower-trimmed hat.

(*right*) As a young wife Madame d'Etioles, née Jeanne Poisson, was surrounded by a gay circle of friends, among them Boucher, to whom she admitted her ambition to become the mistress of King Louis XV. After much intrigue a meeting was arranged at a masked ball, and within a few months she was the titular mistress. In her twenty-third year she was created Marquise de Pompadour and from then until her death sixteen years later she was the most powerful person at court. She was possessed of an extraordinary combination of talents, the capacity for taking infinite pains, and exquisite taste. It is largely due to her that the Sèvres porcelain factory was founded and that artists such as Boucher, who painted this lovely portrait, were given royal encouragement. Her name has become the synonym of perfection in eighteenth century taste.

La Belle O'Morphi was an Irish girl whose father, a shoe-maker, was an adherent of King James II and had settled in Rouen. One of four sisters, another of whom enjoyed Louis XV's favour, the O'Morphi, or "Louison" as she was sometimes called, was brought to Paris after the death of her father, when her mother set up as a second-hand clothes dealer. Her sisters were women of easy virtue and she was not much more than thirteen when in their company she met Casanova, who thought her so pretty that he arranged for her to be painted in the nude. The artist was Boucher, and it was through him that she came to the notice of the King (by whom she had two children) and became one of the earliest occupants of the "Parc aux Cerfs". Her daughter married le Marquis de la Tour du Pin, a distant relative of the famous author of *Le Journal d'une Femme de Cinquante Ans*. O'Morphi is known to have posed for several of Boucher's most famous pictures, including the *Lever* and *Coucher de Vénus*, but this picture is considered the best record of her youthful beauty.

The ladies curled and
powdered their hair until
they looked like

Powdered Poodles

(*above*) The portrait of the Parson's daughter by Romney shows that even an unsophisticated country girl powdered her curls like the ladies of the court: she has also threaded an apple-green ribbon through her mop of hair.

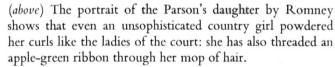

(*left*) Lady Elizabeth Foster was the daughter of the Earl of Bristol, Bishop of Derry, and after she became a widow lived with the Duke and Duchess of Devonshire. Her two children by the Duke were brought up with his legitimate children and three years after the death of the Duchess, she married him. She was painted by Reynolds and, with her slanting eyes and mobile mouth, was accounted a woman of great physical attractions—sly, soft and willing to please, but with few brains.

White curls and pink cheeks are set off by pale satins and snowy muslins tied with brightly coloured ribbons

(*right*) Elizabeth Farren who had a great success on the London stage and was much admired, married the Earl of Derby in 1797 and was one of the first actresses to enter the peerage. Lawrence painted this lovely picture of her in a fur-trimmed satin wrap shortly after her marriage.

(*below*) Mrs. Mark Currie, the Yorkshire bride of a successful banker, was painted in a fashionable white muslin dress with a wide gathered collar and a pink sash, her hair powdered and set in innumerable curls. Her husband commissioned this portrait from Romney and for it paid him sixty-three pounds.

Dressed High

The hair was brushed off the forehead, built up over a frame and powdered or
decorated with pearls and ribbons, and a ringlet was allowed to curl on the neck

The Ladies Waldegrave were painted by Reynolds for their great-uncle Horace Walpole. He had wished them depicted
as the Graces, but his idea was not adopted and they are seen in day costume, embroidering and winding silks. Lady
Laura, afterwards Lady Chewton, is in the middle, Lady Maria is on her right, and Lady Horatia is working at the tambour.

(*above*) Lady Melbourne was the daughter of Sir Ralph Milbanke and was painted by Reynolds when she was one of the great hostesses of London. The rise of the family was due to her brilliant qualities, and her second son, William Lamb, married the wild Caroline Ponsonby and later became the famous Lord Melbourne, Queen Victoria's Prime Minister.

(*above*) The Hon. Mrs. Graham was the daughter of Lord Cathcart, Ambassador at the court of the Tsar, and married a handsome Scottish laird. He was inconsolable at her death, when he turned her portrait to the wall and would never look at it again. She is seen in an elaborate satin dress of soft but glowing colour with a feather trimmed hat perched on her high coiffure. When a critic remarked that the splendour of her attire was the source of her beauty, Gainsborough replied that "she was perfect whichever way I paint her", and to prove it made an enchanting portrait of her dressed as a dairymaid.

(*left*) Reynolds's sketch for the portrait of Mrs. Lloyd, who later married the brother of William Beckford of Fonthill.

(*above*) The Princesse de Lamballe was of mixed Italian and Austrian parentage and was married at eighteen to the Prince de Lamballe, who died soon afterwards. She became a close friend of Marie Antoinette and consequently was one of the first to lose her life in the September massacres of 1792.

(*above*) Madame Vigée-Lebrun received her first lessons in painting from her father, but later studied with Greuze and became a member of the Academy in 1783. She was the favourite painter of Marie Antoinette and made several portraits of the Queen. She also executed many self-portraits, among them the one above in her ravishing garden hat.

(*left*) Madame du Barry was twenty-six when, after a life of gallantry and under a forged birth certificate, she was married to the Comte du Barry and became the King's mistress, a year after the death of the Pompadour. She was to die in the Terror, denounced by her Negro servant, and screaming out the names of her associates in the hope of gaining a reprieve.

The Heavy Head

crowned with
hats, flowers, frills, bonnets
and feathers

(*above*) It was said of Georgiana, Duchess of Devonshire, here painted by Reynolds, that her face "seldom wears and never meets a Frown". She was greatly loved and a contemporary describes her as "the loveliest of the lovelies, the gayest of the gay", yet she managed to contract debts amounting to nearly a hundred thousand pounds and constantly had recourse to her banker "dear Mr. Coutts". Her *ménage à trois* with her great friend Elizabeth Foster (see p. 104) who was also the mistress of her husband and whose illegitimate children were brought up with her own, caused much speculation.

(*left*) Mrs. Mary Robinson was born in America but became a great success on the London stage under the patronage of the Duchess of Devonshire. In the role of Perdita she caught the eye and the heart of the Prince of Wales who gave her a bond for £20,000. It was never honoured and she died in poverty.

A Sweet Disorder

(*right*) "Pale, pretty Pamela", wife of Lord Edward Fitzgerald, was said to be the daughter of Madame de Genlis, governess to the French Royal children, and of the Duc d'Orleans, nicknamed Citoyen Philippe Egalité and brother of Louis XVI. Lord Edward met her when she and Madame de Genlis were refugees from the Terror and married her at Tournai. Although his family loved her dearly, she was obliged to flee from Ireland when he was proscribed as a rebel and spent the rest of her life abroad. Her name has become a synonym for misfortune, but her beauty was transmitted through her daughter Pamela, to be seen again and again in her descendants, among them the Wyndhams and Tennants.

(*left*) When the three daughters of Sir William Montgomery were all engaged to be married, the betrothed of one of them, Luke Gardiner, requested Reynolds to paint the sisters in some emblematic or symbolic manner. Sir Joshua most appropriately depicted them as three Graces decorating the terminal figure of Hymen. This canvas was bequeathed to the National Gallery in London by the Earl of Blessington, a son of Elizabeth, the centre figure in this delightful composition.

110

There are innumerable portraits of Emma Hart, later Lady Hamilton, but perhaps none more felicitous than this by Romney. Emma's charm and distinction endeared her to all who met her and made it possible for her, who started life as a servant girl and passed through several strange vicissitudes, to mix easily with the great. For a time her story became a fairytale in which beauty received all it deserved. Yet in spite of her good marriage, her rich connections and the great love Nelson bore her, she died destitute in a garret in Calais, alone except for Horatia, her daughter by the great admiral.

III

From Nudity to Niceness

The French Revolution found its visual expression in a revival of classic forms and David and Ingres depict a new type of beauty in their models who recline on white and gold Empire furniture. The pink and plump little women of Versailles are replaced by statuesque figures in flimsy white robes, and the intense contrast between nudity and a multiplicity of stiff garments gives way to suggestive draperies which reveal more than they conceal. Long legs are admired, clearly visible through gossamer muslin gowns; great attention is paid to a well-set neck and a well-turned arm, for both are uncovered; and the bosom, barely veiled, is pushed up as high as possible.

The heads, heavy with elaborate coiffures and huge hats, have fallen beneath the guillotine. Now all false additions and powder have disappeared from the hair, which is worn its natural colour, cut short into curls, or parted in the centre and brushed down smoothly. In an age of reason women dream of more emancipated lives; Lady Blessington is known for her books as well as her beauty and soon Caroline Norton will begin her long fight for the rights of married women to retain control over their own property and earnings.

Classic simplicity of dress does not last long and the small corseted waist, now neatly belted, returns to favour. Bosoms are covered and have remained so, but generous décolletages reveal the shoulders and demand huge, sparkling necklaces. Legs disappear beneath spreading skirts and eventually the crinoline makes them as invisible as they are unmentionable. The small woman is again admired, but the "petite femme" returns as the "little lady" whose ringleted coquetry will be recorded so well by Winterhalter and a host of minor Victorian artists. Every limb must be small and fragile, feet silent like "little mice", hands like petals, pale and useless, the nose short and retroussé, the mouth small and rosebud. This is the day of Dora, the child-wife, behind whose domestic and cherished figure lurks the spectre of Dickens' London, and when the tiny figure of a plump

young Queen is revered over one quarter of the globe. The great romantics discover nature, the savage is thought to be "gentle" but must be converted, sins and souls are subjects for conversation, Florence Nightingale brings the word sanitation into daily use, to be followed in due course by the weekly, if not daily, bath. The waltz is danced to the swish of turning crinolines and railways begin to steam their way through the green countryside. Children become fashionable and are taken about by their fond mamas who are now smothered beneath crinolines and shawls.

Nudity ar

(*left*) Madame Recamier was painted by Gerard in the classical robes she helped to launch as a fashion. She was born in Lyons and married a rich banker who brought her to Paris. Later the Imperial Police exiled her from the capital and it was not until the fall of Napoleon that she was allowed to return, when her salon became the centre of a select and literary group, among whom was Chateaubriand, one of her closest friends.

(*below*) Pauline Bonaparte was one of Napoleon's three sisters. She was proud of her beauty and had this portrait sculptured by Canova soon after her marriage to Prince Borghese.

ar Nudity

(*right*) The fashion of representing women as classical charac-
ters was introduced by Sir Joshua Reynolds. Hoppner painted
Lady Heathcote as Hebe. But the classical allusion is no more
than a flattering reference to young beauty, for Hebe is the
goddess of Youth who fills the cups of the gods with nectar.
It was at a ball given by Lady Heathcote that Lady Caroline
Lamb staged her dramatic scene of jealousy with Byron.

(*below*) The Sleeping Nymph was Canova's last work and was
finished by his brother. Its cool perfection recalls a classical
influence that will soon be smothered beneath romantic frills.

(*left*) The Duchess of Vicenza is painted by Prud'hon wearing the short curls fashionable in the first years of the nineteenth century. She was the wife of the Marquis de Caulaincourt, the aristocrat who became Napoleon's great general and diplomatist and for whom he created the Duchy of Vicenza.

(*above*) Lady Caroline Lamb loved to wear page's costume. Slight, ethereal, with curly gold hair, she was the daughter of Lady Bessborough and only seventeen when she married William Lamb, later to be Lord Melbourne and Queen Victoria's trusted first Prime Minister. She was the centre of innumerable scandals. Her affair with Byron was a public sensation and she wrote a book to tell everyone how badly she had been treated. She became more and more hysterical and eccentric, but died when still young and with William still beside her. The miniature from which this illustration is taken is in the possession of Sir John Murray and was given to his great-grandfather by Lord Byron.

(*left*) The pretty Polish Countess Marie Walewska was Napoleon's mistress while he was on his campaign in Russia. She bore him a son who became a minister of Napoleon III.

The Feathered Curl

A delicate frame to small faces and large expressive eyes

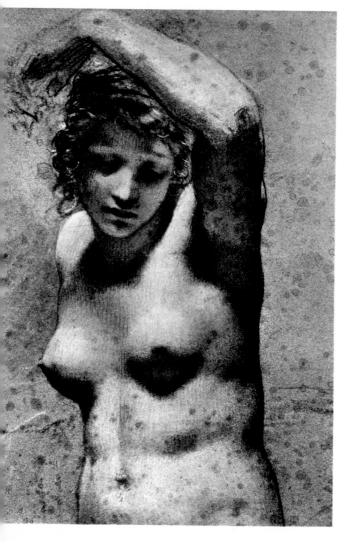

(*above*) Josephine Tascher de la Pagerie was born in Martinique where a native soothsayer told her she would one day be a great Empress. She came to France and married the Vicomte Beauharnais who died on the guillotine, but the young General Bonaparte fell in love with her and in 1796 they married. She became Empress in 1804 but a few years later Napoleon insisted on a divorce in order that he could marry the daughter of the Emperor Francis II of Austria. Josephine was known for her elegance, and the refinement of her taste is reflected in the charming rooms and gardens of Malmaison.

(*left*) This drawing is thought to be of a pupil of Prud'hon's called Constance Mayer. She had a liaison with him for many years, but committed suicide two years before his death.

The apotheosis of the plump woman is superbly illustrated in *The Turkish Bath* by Ingres. Idle nudes pose in every enticing position, and the career woman is still in the far unimaginable future.

Softly Rounded

Every coquetry known to woman is used,
and used daily, by these Spanish beauties:
bright eyes peep over or are
entirely hidden by fluttering fans,
the face is framed by dark curls and
the flattery of lace mantillas veils the hair
and is draped over the full corseted bosom.

(*above*) The full-blown beauty of Doña Isobel de Porcel in Goya's portrait shows a hint of a double chin, arresting eyes, a broad face and a generous bosom swathed in lace.

(*left*) Dark eyes, shadowed by mantillas, were the chief assets of the lovely Majas here painted so seductively by Goya.

The Smooth
Centre Parting

Straight shining hair, neatly banded,
frames the forehead, reveals the
ears and is twisted in a chignon
on the head

(*above*) Madame Devancey's austere good looks painted by
Ingres are an excellent example of the classical restraint soon
to be replaced by the Victoriana of ringlets, frills and flounces.

(*left*) Lord Byron records that when this picture of Lady
Blessington by Lawrence was shown in the Royal Academy of
1821 it "set all London raving". P. G. Patmore, the father of
Coventry Patmore, says as the original stood before it she
"fairly killed the copy" and calls her perhaps the loveliest
woman of her day, while the famous classical scholar,
Doctor Samuel Parr, called her the "most gorgeous". Such
was her impact on London when she and Lord Blessington
first installed themselves in St. James' Square, and she became
as famous for her dinners as for her beauty and wit. Ahead of
her lay the hard work of her many books, distress and the
debts which caused her to fly the country, always in the
company of d'Orsay, the great dandy, who, in his negative
and charming way, was the nemesis of this brilliant woman.

(*right*) Under the pseudonym of "L.E.L.", Letitia Landon published her first poems in the eighteen-twenties. She became a successful writer and earned as much as £2,500 a year. After an unhappy love affair, she married a colonial governor, George MacLean, and was given away by Bulwer Lytton. She died in East Africa from mysterious poisoning.

(*above*) Elizabeth Jennings was one of many lovely and rich young ladies with whom the painter Lawrence's name was coupled. This particular rumour was without foundation but sufficient to cause Sally Siddons, a daughter of the actress and much in love with the seductive artist, a great deal of anguish.

(*right*) Caroline Norton was a brunette with dark burning eyes, a Greek profile and clear olive complexion. She was a grand-daughter of the playwright Sheridan and is remembered not only for the resounding scandal of her first marriage but for the independent manner in which she fought for her rights, which was influential in getting the Married Women's Property Act passed. When she was sixty-nine she married Sir John Stirling Maxwell but died only a few months later.

From a Victorian Keepsake

(*left*) The dripping ringlets, small rosebud mouth and vacant expression of Mrs. Alfred Montgomery are typical of the taste of her time which admired the helpless little woman.

(*above*) The beauty for which the Manners family is remarkable is evident in this charming portrait of Lady John Manners in walking costume, holding a large feathered hat.

(*left*) The immense importance attached to exceptionally long hair is illustrated in this portrait of Mrs. Stanley plaiting her hair. To be able to sit on one's hair was thought a great asset.

(*right*) Georgiana, Duchess of Somerset, was a younger sister of Caroline Norton, and the most beautiful of the three Sheridan sisters who all inherited the charm and intelligence of their grandfather, the well-known playwright. She was elected Queen of Beauty in the famous tournament which cost Lord Eglinton £40,000. Every effort was made to re-create medieval pageantry, knights were trained to joust in full armour, ladies were dressed in the height of Gothic fashion. But on the first day relentless rain fell the whole time and reduced the pageant to a mire.

(*above*) Lady Clementina Villiers allows her long curled locks to hang down below her waist even when formally attired for a ball, and crowns them with a large garland of water-lilies.

(*right*) The baby face of the Viscountess Chesterfield, framed by ringlets and incongruously crowned by a tiara, was painted by Landseer as if she were sitting in her loge at the Opera.

123

The Eclipse
of the Ear

(*left*) Mrs. Sutherland Orr, sister of Lord Leighton, who made this charming drawing of her wearing a ribbon tied crown of leaves, became the biographer of Robert Browning.

(*below*) Ophelia sinking beneath the water level is carried away by a bevy of nymphs in this English painting done in the year of the Great Exhibition, 1851. No matter what else their flowing draperies may reveal, each and every one has her ears carefully covered by her long tresses.

Smooth dark hair, uniformly parted in the centre, was brushed down to cover the ears and worn in a large knot at the back of the head: a smooth brow and a calm expression were cultivated, and the eyebrows clearly defined.

(*above*) The beautiful sisters, Lady Waterford and Lady Canning, attracted universal admiration. Louisa's soft blonde beauty contrasted admirably with the dark hair and pensive grace of Charlotte, and when they entered a room together every eye was turned to them. They were painted thus in a miniature by Thorburn. Lady Waterford, an enthusiastic and talented artist, was widowed quite young and spent the rest of her life between her Border castle and Highcliffe, the medieval house brought over from France by their father, Lord Stuart de Rothesay, and put up on the Hampshire cliffs. Lady Canning died of jungle fever in India when she was Vicereine, at the time of the Indian Mutiny.

(*left*) Lola Montez was said by contemporaries to possess twenty-six of the twenty-seven points considered essential to feminine beauty. A mediocre dancer of Irish extraction, she knew well how to entrance all who saw her but her greatest conquest was Ludwig I of Bavaria. Her success did not last long and she soon had to leave the country, never again to move in such exalted circles. She went to the far West of America and in later life became an enthusiastic Evangelist.

The Vogue for Ringlets

(*above left*) This portrait of Queen Alexandra was drawn by W. P. Frith on her wedding day, and was a sketch for his official painting. He gave it to the Duchess of Teck, and it is now in the possession of Her Majesty the Queen.

(*below left*) The Duchesse de Morny was born Princess Sophie Troubetskoie and met her husband when he was Ambassador in Russia. She caused a sensation when she first appeared in Paris. She and her friend, the Princess Pauline Metternich, were the originators of many of the fancy dress balls and tableaux vivants which enlivened the court.

(*below right*) Vicomtesse Aquado, Marquise de las Marismas, was one of the six ladies-in-waiting chosen to attend on the new Empress when Eugénie de Montijo married Napoleon III. Her spaniel-like ringlets accentuate the oval of her face and her large, expressive eyes in this portrait by Winterhalter.

No woman ever knew better how to adorn herself than Eugénie de Montijo the beautiful Spaniard who became Empress of the French. Her perfect taste in dress is recorded in many memoirs and Winterhalter delighted to paint her.

127

Two Great Beauties of the Nineteenth Century

The Countess of Cardigan attracted a good deal of attention when, still Miss Horsey de Horsey, she rode in the Park with Lord Cardigan, of Balaclava fame, then a married man. Though she married again after his death and was said to be as gay and unconventional in her old age as she had been in her youth, she greatly venerated the memory of her first husband and kept his uniform, together with the stuffed head of his charger in the front hall of their house. His flair for clothes gave the English wardrobe two indispensable items still often worn today, the cardigan and the balaclava helmet.

The Reign of Tarleton, Barège, Grenadine and Gauze

Those who knew the Empress Elizabeth of Austria-Hungary said she was not only unbelievably beautiful but extremely graceful, with a lovely swaying walk, and that even Winterhalter's romantic portrait did not do her justice. She was a younger daughter of the house of Wittlesbach and her elder sister was destined for the Archduke Franz-Joseph, but she set herself to fascinate and eventually married him. But the marriage led to a life of tragedy; her only son, the Archduke Rudolph, shot himself in the sensational drama of Mayerling, and she herself was stabbed to death.

(*above*) The Comtesse de Castiglione's beauty so overcame an English statesman not very conversant with French that he said: "Madame, vous êtes éclaboussante." She was born in Florence, married when only fifteen and was left a widow at an early age. Cavour, who was her cousin, sent her to Paris in order to have a friend at the French court and she captivated the heart of Napoleon III. She delighted in masquerade balls and was frequently photographed in fancy dress—but never more strangely than in this photograph, one of the earliest known *trompe l'oeil* effects of the camera. Already one can discern the discontent which made her mouth curl downwards and caused her to retire voluntarily from the world. She spent the last thirty years of her life secluded in her Paris flat, only going out at night, heavily veiled, so that none could see her fading beauty.

(*right*) Classic in its pure outline but romantic in the spirit which informs it, is this painting by Couture of a recumbent nude.

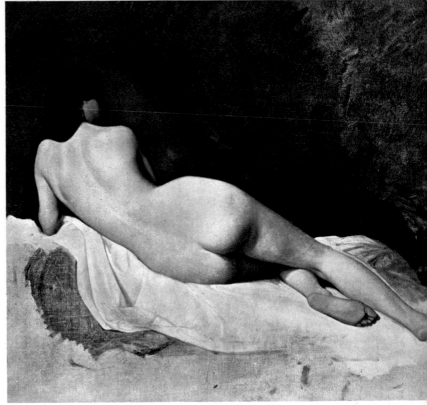

Romantic Dreamers

(*above*) Louise, Duchess of Manchester, was born Countess Frederica von Alten and was mistress of the robes to Queen Victoria. She married her second husband, the Duke of Devonshire, when she was sixty, and lived almost until the outbreak of the First World War. Thorburn painted her in the 1850's as a vision of loveliness on a moon-lit balcony.

(*left*) Among the many creamy nudes for which Ingres is famous perhaps none is more successful than this calm Aphrodite painted in the middle of the century and towards the end of his long career. She rises from the waves, where rosy cherubs gambol around her feet, wringing the water from her fair hair. Her pale perfection reflects the same silhouette and romantic calm as the dreaming Duchess of Manchester.

Revolt & Counter-revolt

The Pre-Raphaelite painters evolved a new type of woman. The curls, rosebud mouth and innocent eyes of the demure Victorian miss are forgotten. Heavy wings of hair shadow mournful eyes and full lips are exaggeratedly sculptured. Beautiful women are referred to as "stunners" but they are also symbols in which mysticism is allied to sensuality, a theme developed by Rossetti in his many portraits of his wife, of the exotic Mrs. William Morris, and of Alice Wildman. These strangely beautiful women, one a milliner's assistant, one a groom's daughter and the third a professional model, are given fanciful names and dressed in trailing robes. But even when entitled "Venus" they are covered from throat to toe, for this is a period when a patron was disquieted by the sight of a bare arm, when Burne-Jones resigned from the Royal Academy because a picture was rejected on the grounds of its being a nude, and when Ruskin assured his students that the study of anatomy was "not only a hindrance but a degradation".

The chief interest in these portraits is centred in the huge eyes and what Swinburne called "those terrible lips", in the almost goitrous necks, and above all in the hair, which often flows unconfined over the shoulders. This lack of artifice contrasts strikingly with the ringlets and fringes of the more bourgeoise, whose crinolines have also been discarded, for no hoops support the full skirts of the Pre-Raphaelite women. Medievalism was the *beau idéal* and the Knights of the Round Table were familiar to the young artists; they read out loud to each other Malory's *Morte d'Arthur* and were overwhelmed by the weirdness of the Maids of Elfinmere. At fancy dress balls aristocratic ladies were attired in historical costumes and a knight in armour was considered an essential decoration for a successful artist's studio. The style the Pre-Raphaelites developed had astonishingly enduring results and women with long skirts and strings of out-landish beads around their necks did not disappear finally until the "Tidy Twenties" put an end to romanticism. When a counter-revolt set in the Impressionists painted women whose fresh and dew-like beauty caused a sensation, and the nude triumphed once more, only to be overstated by official art and dissolved by the Cubists early in the next century. In the meantime the height of beauty once again consists of a well-turned waist, a fine bust and curled hair. With the corset, the ruffles and the ribbons, the eyes become calm and tender, the mouth soft and small, the hands and arms plump. We have come out of the mists of medievalism into the comfort of a plush-upholstered drawing-room.

Rossetti's
Models

(*above*) Elizabeth Siddall was a milliner's apprentice and lived with Rossetti for several years before they regularized their union, but she was never at ease in her new surroundings and ended her life of brooding melancholy and ill-health by her own hand. This tragedy left an enduring mark on Rossetti who loved to draw her sad face. With her complexion which was said to look as if a wild rose lay beneath the white skin, her heavy dark red hair, and tall slender figure, she was the "incarnate opposite of the tailor-made young lady".

(*left*) The strange beauty of Jane Burden, who became William Morris's wife, had a great influence on the Pre-Raphaelite Brotherhood. The tangled threads of her relationship with Rossetti have never been unwound, but she posed for him continuously, and the idyll of their life at Kelmscott when Morris was in Iceland is enshrined in many poems and pictures. This is possibly his earliest drawing of her. Later Henry James spoke of her thin, pale face and pair of deep, dark Swinburnian eyes shadowed by thick, black, oblique brows.

134

*Huge melancholy eyes, shadowed by
heavy wings of hair, deeply sculptured lips and
swan-like necks are all common to these portraits
of four different women who
by some miraculous fate
appeared before the painter's eyes and
gave bodily substance to his dreams.*

(*above*) Alice Wildman, a favourite model of Rossetti's later years, whom he met in a casual encounter, sat for this imaginary portrait of *Monna Vanna*. Her streaming hair, rich apparel and peacock's fan are all typical of the false medievalism then the vogue and she appears in many famous pictures.

(*left*) Miss Herbert, a well-known actress then playing at the St. James's Theatre, aroused great enthusiasm among the Pre-Raphaelites who met at Mrs. Prinsep's house in Holland Park. Here Rossetti has painted her head with its radiant golden hair caught in a mesh against an emerald green background.

The Cult of Long Hair

Hair assumes the importance of a fetish and is valued in relation to its length and volume: women brushing and plaiting their hair become a favourite subject for artist and camera.

(*above*) The Empress Elizabeth of Austria was enormously proud of her hair which she usually wore in great loops on her neck, but in this portrait by Winterhalter she displays its full length. The ritual of her toilette was elaborate and she was known for the attention she gave to its minute details.

(*right*) Vita Sackville-West published this charming photograph in her book *Pepita*, which told the fascinating story of her mother's life, of how a Spanish gipsy dancer married an English aristocrat and what happened to them afterwards—a love-story as extraordinary as the most romantic novel. This photograph of her brushing her long hair was taken in Washington when Lord Sackville was in the Embassy there during the 'nineties. Later Lady Sackville became the mistress of Knole, the immense Tudor mansion of the Sackvilles in Kent, and one of the largest private residences in Europe.

(*above*) This is one of several pictures Courbet painted of *Jo, la Belle Irlandaise* attending to her rippling auburn hair.

(*above*) Fanny Cornforth, plaiting her "harvest-yellow hair" was the model for this fanciful portrait of *Aurelia*. It is said that Rossetti met her in the streets and she was certainly the model for *Found*. She posed for innumerable pictures but her heavy nose and mouth and thick throat became coarse as she grew older, though her long and varied personal association with Rossetti lasted almost until his death.

(*left*) The theme of a woman doing her hair was particularly attractive to Courbet, and its charm and the atmosphere of the period could not be evoked more clearly than in this picture of a young woman seated before her flounced dressing table.

Post-
Pre-Raphaelites

Memories of an idealised past are recalled by these women with lowered eyes and straight hair simply arranged, whose picturesque draperies are derived from those of fifteenth century Sybils.

(*above*) The favourite model of the "Signor", as Watts was nicknamed, was photographed by Mrs. Cameron, who gave a signed life-size print to the artist, from which this reproduction was taken. Beatrice, as she is inevitably called, is shown with her head draped and a demure expression in imitation of Raphael and the painters who preceded him.

(*right*) The late nineteenth century revived the long-forgotten fashion for the draped head and downcast glance, and here the Venetian painter Francesco Hoyez, a master of the romantic style, shows a contemporary version of an Odalisque, complete with draperies, modestly holding up her robes.

These two lovely girls with tender dreamy expressions, their hair flowing freely and wearing unfashionable dresses, illustrate a brief interlude when the revolt of an artistic minority attempted to emancipate women from the tyranny of over-curled hair and over-elaborate, corseted clothes.

(*above*) This exquisite portrait of Ellen Terry was painted by Watts soon after she married the artist and just before her seventeenth birthday. She is shown in her wedding gown, designed by Holman Hunt, drawing towards her a scentless camellia, while in her left hand she holds some violets. The title is *Choosing* and the symbolism may be obscure, but no one can be unaware of the breathless vision of loveliness which Watts perpetuated of the beautiful girl-wife who was so soon to leave him, but who later became one of the greatest actresses the world has ever known.

(*left*) When most women were upholstered in heavy fabrics and their heads top-heavy with chignons, Whistler's *Little White Girl* with her simple dress and long hair caused a stir.

139

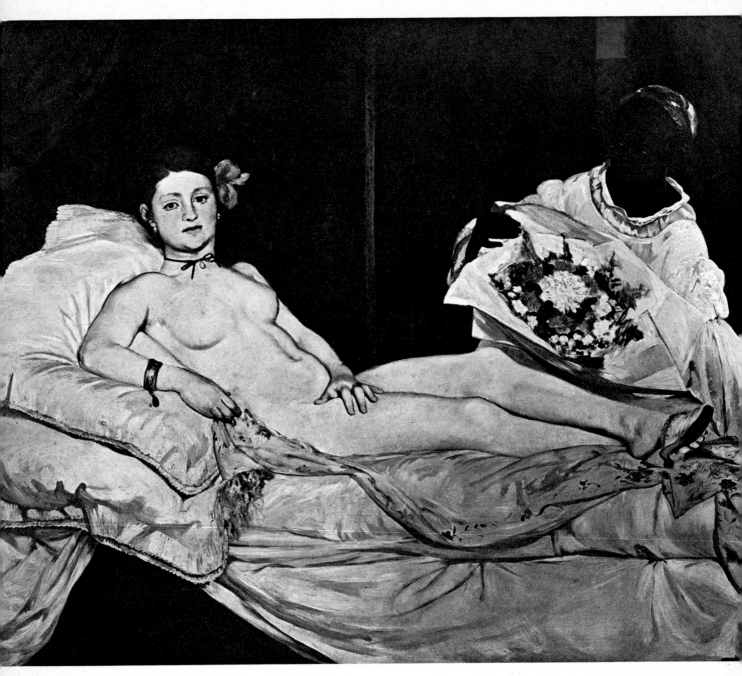

Although her pose is classic and has been seen again and again in the past, this nude Olympia proclaims the date of her appearance by the black ribbon tied around her throat and the wide gold bracelet on her arm. She created a sensation when Manet first exhibited her at the Paris Salon.

Dressed & Undressed in the 'Eighties

A round face, plump neck and full high bosom were admired, but the generous figure was constricted by miracles of corsetry into the fashionable shape of an hour-glass: embroideries and lace decorated the plush and satin gowns until a woman resembled a sugar-sweet in a be-ribboned bonbonnière.

(*above*) An outstanding example of what fashion can do: compare the waist and figure of young Madame Michel-Levy, painted by Manet in her elegant afternoon dress of plush, satin and lace, with that of Renoir's nude. The corseted bodice with its ruffles forms a frame for the plump throat.

(*left*) Renoir's *Jeune fille* shows well the rounded flesh and long hair admired by the Impressionists, whose women were of a more solid build than their mid-Victorian predecessors, though less statuesque than their Edwardian daughters. Heavy eyebrows characterise both these portraits.

141

In this study for the painting *Too Early* by Tissot, the young lady is complete with bustle, fan and ribbon-tied gloves, a feather in her curled hair, a black velvet band round her neck.

Berthe Morisot, the most gifted woman artist of her epoch, pupil and sister-in-law of Manet, painted this delightful picture of a woman dressed in her elaborate evening toilette.

142

This unknown beauty leans against a green sofa, then the colour *à la mode* in decoration. Her round chin, arched eyebrows and plump neck and bosom framed by lace flounces are recorded with the utmost felicity by Berthe Morisot, who excelled in depicting her fashionably dressed contemporaries.

Official Art

in Paris at the turn of the century,
when the ample proportions of the nymphs
reflect the fashionable sway-back.

(*opposite*) A splendid example of academic art at its most exuberant: *Les Oréades* by Bouguereau was much admired when it was exhibited in the 'nineties.

(*above*) The bustle was added to dresses in order to enhance the importance of the posterior: this frieze exhibited in the Paris Salon clearly shows that nature was expected to follow the demands of art.

(*left*) The S-shaped figure decreed by fashion and achieved by corsetry is well displayed in this nude statue of Cleo de Mérode, the famous *demi-mondaine*. Her pose recalls the fifteenth century sway-back, but her figure is definitely far more ample than that of any medieval girl.

1900
The Turn of a Century

Hydrangeas are the favourite flower and wistaria the chosen colour. Kings are still on all the thrones of Europe except France. The invasion of the aristocracy by American heiresses has begun and with their arrival the emancipation of women becomes more than a subject for discussion. It is the day of *Grand Ducs* and great beauties, when people stand on chairs to see the Jersey Lily pass in the Park, when Liane de Pougy's long trains billow behind her in the streets of Paris, La Belle Otero wears her magnificent rows of pearls like a native woman her rings of copper, and Loie Fuller enchants everyone with her scarf dance. Cleo de Mérode, jealous of the newly-arrived Javanese dancers, wears innumerable jewelled serpents and is admired by Anatole France. Sarah Bernhardt's golden voice echoes in the theatre where Henry Irving's *Bells* will soon be ringing. Reynaldo Hahn's pale melodies are beginning to be heard. Marcel Proust is writing in secret and, unheralded, Pablo Picasso arrives in Paris from the Ecole des Beaux-Arts in Barcelona. New methods and great techniques are used for trivial purposes, art-nouveau bends and twists every object of daily life but congeals as the entry to the Metro in Paris. Rodin exhibits in Paris for the first time, but Bouguereau is the popular painter.

Whistler has thrown his pot of paint in the public's face and the aesthetic movement, spiritual descendant of the Pre-Raphaelites and William Morris, has declined, the Souls have abandoned their draperies. The willowy aesthetes appear to have given birth to a race of goddesses. Could Brünnhilde's war-cries ringing out in the world's opera houses have influenced the mothers of this generation? Are Wagnerian ideals to be held responsible for these magnificent women, or is this period under the special care of Juno? Splendid bosoms, more than amply displayed, are counter-balanced by a backward movement of large hips and buttocks in an S-shape, reminiscent of the medieval illustrators, but now joined by a waist so small that but for its steel girder of corset one feels

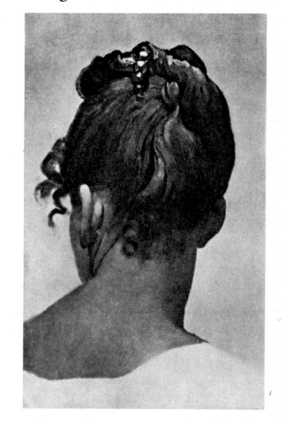

it would snap. Fine shoulders are a necessity for the would-be beauty, the shrinking lass with the delicate air has entirely vanished and the Gibson Girl is the toast of two continents. Necks are referred to as "columns" and look like them. Legs are not referred to at all, but feet peep out under all the frou-frous of innumerable flounced petticoats in pointed satin shoes or patent leather buttoned boots. This is the period when tennis is played in long skirts and straw hats, when chinchilla is the favourite fur, and when "high life" became a French phrase as well as a European reality.

147

Jennie Jerome (*above, left*) was the daughter of the fabulous millionaire Leonard Jerome of New York and the mother of Winston Churchill. She married first Lord Randolph Churchill and later became Mrs. George Cornwallis West.

Mary Wemyss (*below, left*), daughter of Percy Scawen Wyndham and a descendant of Pamela Fitzgerald, married the Earl of Wemyss in the 'eighties, not long before this charming drawing was made. Her daughter, Lady Cynthia Asquith, carries on the family tradition of beauty and wit.

Lady Sybil St. Clair Erskine (*above, right*) married the Earl of Westmorland in the 'nineties, when she was sketched by the talented Marchioness of Granby, later well-known as Violet, Duchess of Rutland, who executed the drawings on this page.

Norah Lindsay (*below, right*), sister-in-law of the artist, often wore classical robes and a wreath of laurel leaves in her hair, dressed in a Grecian knot. She was, said a contemporary, "quite exquisitely lovely". Later she was to become famous as a gardener and she has left a legacy of real beauty behind her.

Fringes

(*above*) Lily Langtry was the only daughter of a clergyman in Jersey. She made a run-away marriage with an Englishman when very young, but the union did not last long. Then with the help of Sir Squire and Lady Bancroft she went on the stage and was an immediate success, and was soon taken up by the Prince of Wales. This portrait by Watts was painted at about the time she first appeared in London when the gossip writer of *The World* spoke of her " dewy violet eyes, a complexion like a peach, and a mass of lovely hair ".

(*left*) Alice Meynell was one of two gifted sisters—the other was Lady Butler, famous as a war artist. At an early age she began to write poems which attracted the attention and praise of Ruskin. Her marriage to Wilfred Meynell and the birth of her children brought her great happiness, and her friendship with Francis Thompson is now part of literary history. In this drawing by Sargent the gentleness and compassion for which she was known are clearly written on her face.

Three of Pamela Fitzgerald's (see p. 110) descendants who inherited her beauty were the daughters of Percy Scawen Wyndham. Sargent painted them when they were Mrs. Adeane, Mrs. Tennant (later Lady Glenconner) and Lady Elcho (later the Countess of Wemyss). The centre figure, Pamela Tennant, was named after her famous great-grandmother.

Elegant Airs

Straight backs and long necks
support small heads piled high
with curled hair

(*above*) The Comtesse Henri Greffulhe was not only one of
the most famous beauties in Paris but a brilliant woman
whose salon was frequented by writers and wits. It was said
that she would be known as the Récamier of her time. Marcel
Proust was dazzled by her at their first meeting and made her
the model for Madame de Guermantes in his great novel.

(*left*) Alexandra, " sea-king's daughter from over the sea ",
was the eldest daughter of King Christian of Denmark and
married the Prince of Wales, who was to become Edward VII.
She was known for her rose-petal complexion, and later in
life for her very personal coiffure. " Alexandra " fringes and
dog-collars became a universal fashion followed for many years.

(*left*) Consuelo Vanderbilt's unusual beauty caused a sensation when she married the Duke of Marlborough at Blenheim.

(*above*) Marie, the last Queen of Roumania, a grand-daughter both of Queen Victoria and of the Czar Alexander II, was born in England. She was extremely popular in her adopted country, but saw the end of the monarchy and her son deposed.

(*left*) Cleo de Mérode, a celebrated actress and courtesan, was reputed to have had an injury to one of her ears: hence her adherence to a coiffure which covered them closely. Her huge hat and wide velvet neckband are redolent of the period.

152

(*right*) The famous American actress Mrs. Brown Potter, painted by Lavery, was one of the best dressed women of her day.

(*above*) Anna de Noailles was drawn as a young woman by Helleu and his attractive portrait was modestly entitled " the author of *Coeur inombrable*," an early novel by the famous poetess, written when she was comparatively unknown.

(*right*) The Viscountess Curzon, later Countess Howe, was a typical English rose, with pink and white complexion, blue eyes and golden hair, here well set off by a froth of ostrich feathers. Her son is the well-known racing motorist, Earl Howe.

Rustling Silks

A frou-frou of taffeta
and a swirl of chiffon

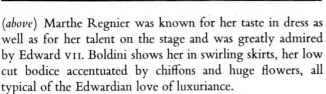

(*above*) Marthe Regnier was known for her taste in dress as well as for her talent on the stage and was greatly admired by Edward VII. Boldini shows her in swirling skirts, her low cut bodice accentuated by chiffons and huge flowers, all typical of the Edwardian love of luxuriance.

(*right*) Princess Marthe Bibesco, a Roumanian by birth, wrote her first book when she was eighteen. She received a prize for it from the Académie Française—the youngest author ever to receive the honour. She is shown here, painted *con brio* by Boldini, at the height of her exuberant beauty.

At a time when large, important looking women were much admired, Consuelo Vanderbilt, the young American who became Duchess of Marlborough, won all hearts against all the rules with her small heart-shaped face. Boldini painted her with her son Ivor. To-day, as Madame Balsan, her beauty is as legendary as her taste and elegance.

Up-swept Hair

Fine necks support clear-cut features
and heads are piled high
with luxuriant hair

(*above*) Frances, Countess of Warwick, was one of the most admired figures at the court of King Edward, of whom she was an intimate friend. In later life she became an ardent Socialist, devoted her life to the cause, and made her house the centre of a group of enlightened politicians and thinkers.

(*right*) Lady de Grey, previously the Countess of Lonsdale and later the Marchioness of Ripon, is remembered for her beauty, wit and sharp repartee. She was an active and discriminating patroness of opera and music, a friend of Nellie Melba and of Oscar Wilde, and the mother of Lady Juliet Duff.

The Mono-bosom

A splendid figure and generous
décolletage were essential to
all Edwardian beauties

(*above*) Millicent, Duchess of Sutherland was famous for her
gaiety, charm and immense vitality. In the First World War
she started a hospital in Northern France and worked in it
herself. There she met and married a handsome young officer
considerably her junior. Her portrait was painted by Sargent.

(*left*) The long neck and delicate features of Helen Dun-
combe, who became Viscountess d'Abernon, were considered perfection by her contemporaries, and are exquisitely
shown in this portrait by Sargent. Her deep décolletage and
silk wrap form a splendid frame for her bare shoulders.

The Gibson Girl

(*left*) In this portrait of Madame Gautreau, Sargent gives his version of the so-called Gibson Girl—bare shoulders, large bust, small boned waist and a noticeable hour-glass silhouette.

(*below*) Miss Camille Clifford was a Gaiety Girl and the most famous exponent of the Gibson Girl cult—mono-bosomed, S-shaped figure and her head crowned by a mountain of hair.

Soft Plumage

The cherished young woman in the first decade of this century was proud of her prominent bosom and hand-span waist and liked the coquetry of feathers and furs.

Helleu delighted in drawing the fashionably dressed women of his day and has left enchanting records of their taste. For the high-piled hair a toque was the chosen companion, often of fur and always trimmed with feathers or flowers and skewered to the coiffure by alarming hat-pins. No head-gear was better adapted to showing off a clear-cut profile.

Maxine Elliott, an American whose sister married the famous actor-manager Sir John Forbes-Robertson, made a name for herself in the theatre but retired early to the South of France. She made an immediate conquest of King Edward VII when she met him at Baden and is remembered affectionately by all who knew her for her warm vitality and striking good looks.

When too much was barely sufficient . . .

(above) Gaby Deslys, the exotic French star, appeared at the Gaiety in 1906 and was billed as the Charm of Paris. Later she went into management with her famous partner, Harry Pilcer, and J. M. Barrie wrote a revue for her called *Rosy Rapture*. In this drawing Drian shows her wearing the abundant ropes of pearls and huge extravagant plumes typical of the costumes which made her famous.

(*below*) La Belle Otero was the daughter of a Spanish gipsy. She was applauded and admired wherever she went in those last years of extravagance before the First World War. Her life was a long series of improbable abductions and adventures with Spanish grandees, French Counts, German Barons and Russian Princes and her rival passions, jewels and gambling, ruined most of her many lovers—though all were undoubtedly rich.

(*right*) Lina Cavalieri began her career in a Café Chantant at the Folies Bergère but she became famous as an opera singer. *Manon Lescaut* and *Tosca* were two of her favourite roles and in both her own ravishing beauty added to the charm of her performance. She had a great sense of the dramatic: once she appeared in Rome dressed entirely in black, driving in an open carriage drawn by black horses, and with a white ermine rug over her knees. Her slender figure and gentle beauty were a striking contrast to the monumental prima donnas with small claim to looks who were her rivals.

(*below*) Mademoiselle Lantêlme was another French actress famous for her beauty in the nineteen-hundreds. Her clothes and her jewels, her rooms and her pet griffons, were all the talk of Paris. She was the mistress of the millionaire newspaper proprietor Alfred Edwards, and his wife Missia Sert, wrote a far from friendly account of their liaison. Lantêlme's career as a *demi-mondaine* ended when she was drowned in rather mysterious circumstances from the yacht of her lover.

The Figure deflates, the Hair descends

(*above*) This wan and slender waif, painted by Picasso in 1905, is coiffed in the fashion of her day; but in all other respects she is twenty years ahead of her time. Only then will the world suddenly become full of similar *chétif* young women. As usual art comes first and nature copies as best she may.

(*right*) The Princess Patricia of Connaught was a descendant of Catherine the Great of Russia and a granddaughter of Queen Victoria. This portrait of her as a young girl was painted by J. J. Shannon and shows her with her hair on top of her head and her waist corseted—both fashions soon to be discarded.

(*above*) Gina Palerme first appeared on the stage during the First World War in the revue *Bric-à-Brac* with Teddy Gerrard and Gertie Miller and made a great impression with her large violet-coloured eyes and fair curls falling on her shoulders.

(*right*) A nude with a slender straight up and down figure comes as a startling change from the taste—and the approved feminine form—of the previous century. Bonnard's natural young woman, without exaggerated waist or protuberant bust and with her hair down is a newcomer to the scene.

163

The Curtained Forehead

(*above*) A high forehead shadowed by looped-up hair, a fine bone structure and classic features distinguish Mrs. Saxton, now Lady Noble and mother of Lady Jebb, British Ambassadress in Paris. She was a great London hostess in the early decades of this century and her musical salon was famous.

(*left*) At the Gaiety Theatre in London in the early years of this century Rosie Boote sang a famous musical comedy number called "Maisie" which drew the whole town. She rose from this performance into the peerage. Orpen painted this portrait soon after she became the Marchioness of Headfort.

164

Loops of straight or softly waved
hair frame oval faces
and partly cover the ears,
from which sometimes hang
long dangling ear-rings

(*above*) Lily Elsie was a typical English Rose and her gentle tender expression and classic features are a far cry from the boyish girls of succeeding generations. She is best remembered as "The Merry Widow" and "The Dollar Princess" in musical comedies at Daly's under George Edwards' inspired management, and with Joe Coyne as her Ruritanian partner.

(*left*) Violet Lindsay, later Duchess of Rutland, is here seen painted by Shannon but she was herself no mean portraitist. She has left many charming records of her friends and contemporaries and she particularly loved to record the beauty of her youngest daughter, now Lady Diana Cooper.

Recent History

The most dramatic change in women's looks for over a hundred years, and one of the most startling in the whole history of beauty, now takes place. The Edwardian bosom is replaced by a flat chest, and the opulent S-shape of the Gibson Girl by a skinny figure which would have been the despair of the previous generation.

The early 'twenties see the last of the magnificent Poiret fancy-dress balls, but Van Dongen still gives his studio parties frequented by slender wraiths in chiffon shifts, their kohl-rimmed eyes set in pale faces. The forehead, for a time completely hidden by hair, hats or swathed turbans, timidly reappears until it is revealed completely by the revolutionary Eton crop. The shape of the head, unseen for generations, becomes important, ears and neck are unsoftened by chignons or ringlets, and after years of an iron rule, the symmetrical ridges of marcel-waved hair disappear. Hair is first straight but then becomes an unruly mop of permanent curls. The cropped head attempts to give an illusion of nudity and this is enhanced by the pale coloured dresses whose fluttering petal skirts barely cover the knee. Legs are visible for the first time for centuries and flesh-

166

coloured stockings make them appear naked. Magnificent jewellery has vanished with the generous bosom and only long ropes of beads or pearls hang on the flattened chests.

Ballroom dancing is the craze and its exponents, Mrs. Vernon Castle and Leonora Hughes, the stars of their day whose every gesture and costume is admired and copied. The slender silhouette of the women is repeated in the lines of Corbusier's City Towers; African art becomes fashionable and Negro masks appear in the best drawing rooms, where jazz is the chosen music and everyone dances the Charleston. The "Blackbirds" troupe of coloured dancers electrify London, and the magic of their rhythm and, later, the streamlined body of Josephine Baker offer a new and exotic type of beauty, which for the first time looks outside Europe for its inspiration.

As the Dancing 'Twenties give way to the Ladylike 'Thirties a different and quieter tempo of life evolves. Garbo's face fills the cinemas of the world with her incomparable beauty; too universal to set a fashion, she represents all and everything to everyone. As smoothly cropped heads become smothered in curls, eyes and mouth lose their prime importance and eyebrows are allowed to form a

natural arc over lightly maquilled eyes. Hair reaches the shoulders, which are squarely padded; uneven hem lines nearly reach the ankles; one-piece corselettes flatten bust and waist. And after the craze for all-white rooms, Regency decoration is now de rigueur, although long-despised Victoriana is beginning to be thought amusing.

Total Eclipse

The forehead is entirely hidden
by hair, hats or turbans;
all the emphasis is on the large,
heavily accentuated eyes

(*above*) Hazel Lavery was considered the ideal Irish colleen and her husband, Sir John Lavery, painted her many times. Her wide-eyed beauty is capable of withstanding even the rigours of early 'twenties millinery and is immortalised in the head engraved from a drawing of Sir John's on the Irish pound note.

(*left*) The legendary looks of the Manners family were inherited in a spectacular degree by Lady Diana Cooper. Her translucent skin and large, light blue eyes and serene expression made her a sensation when she played the role of the Madonna in Reinhardt's never-to-be-forgotten production of *The Miracle*.

(*right*) One of the early "vamps" of the cinema, Pola Negri made a great success when Pomner directed her in *Hotel Imperial* in the middle 'twenties. She played the lead in *One Arabian Night*, considered Ernst Lubitsch's masterpiece.

(*above*) The intense gaze of Theda Bara's huge dark eyes is shadowed by her long hair which she wears bound round her forehead. She was one of the earliest stars of the screen and took herself and her roles very seriously indeed.

(*right*) This is Gloria Swanson as she appeared as a *femme fatale* in *Don't Change Your Husband* in 1921 at the beginning of her long career on the screen. Eyes were then the most important feature and her forehead and hair are shrouded in mystery and the then fashionable turban of gold lamé.

169

The Forehead Reappears

(*below*) Maria Ricotti's success on the Paris stage in *L'Enjoleuse* owed a good deal to her slick dark looks. She popularised the "bob", precursor of the shingle, and had her large eyes heavily made up. She was painted several times by Van Dongen.

(*above*) The huge eyes, smooth heavy eye-lids darkened by shadows and perfectly drawn mouth of Paula Gellibrand, the famous beauty who became the Marquise de Casa Maury, were an excellent foil to the new fashion of short hair which, for the first time in a decade, revealed the forehead.

(*above*) Clara Bow was known as the "It" girl to her numerous admirers in the 'twenties. In her day she was the biggest box-office draw in the cinema and no other "flapper" was thought to dance the Charleston quite so well.

Gladys Cooper represents the typical beauty of blonde hair and blue eyes but adds to it an unusually large leavening of intelligence. One of her early successes was in *My Lady's Dress* in the 'twenties when this photograph was taken. After many years of delighting us on the stage she is now as much at home on the screen as in the theatre.

The Dancing
Twenties

(*above*) Gabrielle Chanel, known to her friends as Coco, is the woman who gave the word "casual" to fashion. In the 'twenties, she built up, from very small beginnings, one of the world's most famous dress houses and her "little" jersey dresses were nothing short of revolutionary to a generation used to corsets, and her exquisite taste in decoration is equally original. Marie Laurencin painted her with one of her famous scarves, the first of their kind, wound round her neck.

(*right*) Mrs. Vernon Castle and her husband were the most famous ballroom dancers of the days when *thé-dansants* were the rage and the tango the newest step. Her elegance made her a great influence in the world of fashion and she led where others followed. These gay and vivacious sketches of her were drawn by Drian when she was at the height of her fame.

The vamp has vanished: corsets are off and
hair is cut; small heads with marcel-waved hair
top slender figures in chiffon sheaths.
Light of heart and light in weight,
everyone dances to Alexander's Ragtime Band.

(*above*) Leonora Hughes floated rather than danced; she and her partner Maurice were the great attractions of the well-known London night-club the "Embassy" and of the "Jardin de ma Soeur" in Paris. Jean Patou, the great couturier was at the summit of his success, and dressed her exquisitely in pale colours and fragile sheaths and Baron de Meyer photographed her against a background of shimmering light. She married a South American and retired to live in the Argentine.

(*left*) This is a period when for once waists are forgotten and the vital statistics must all closely approximate for their owner to be a candidate for beauty. Hips are flat, bosoms negligible and bare backs the focus of attention. Van Dongen paints Mrs. Forrester Agar with the then fashionable no-bust, no-waist line accentuated by a long diamond necklace.

173

Neat and Tidy

The shingled head
and the painted face

(*above*) This *Vogue* cover of 1926 by Benito illustrates clearly
the contemporary ideal of smooth boyish freshness: the short
hair carefully brushed into a neat Eton crop, the ears exposed,
the eyes and mouth outlined and accentuated.

(*right*) The mother of the Hon. Mrs. Reginald Fellowes was
the American Miss Singer and her father was the Duc de
Breteuil. Her neat, well-groomed, good looks were well
attuned to the tidy 'twenties when Manray photographed her,
but her remarkable flair both for clothes and for interior
decoration would have been equal to any period. The house
which she recently furnished in Strawberry Hill Gothic
has done much to restore to fashion that once neglected style.

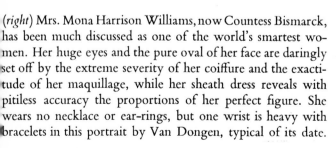

(*above*) Kay Francis, a young actress who made a considerable mark when she first appeared, was painted by Sir Gerald Kelly in 1925 wearing the simple sheath dress of lamé—almost an evening uniform that year. Her hair is shingled and very short.

(*right*) Mrs. Mona Harrison Williams, now Countess Bismarck, has been much discussed as one of the world's smartest women. Her huge eyes and the pure oval of her face are daringly set off by the extreme severity of her coiffure and the exactitude of her maquillage, while her sheath dress reveals with pitiless accuracy the proportions of her perfect figure. She wears no necklace or ear-rings, but one wrist is heavy with bracelets in this portrait by Van Dongen, typical of its date.

175

Prettiness and Pathos

Even in its heyday the rule of the Marcel Wave was never undisputed; and fringes, both straight and curled, reappear after a generation of neglect

(*above*) The slight but rounded figure which was admired in the 'thirties is charmingly illustrated in this pretty nude by Kisling with her thick dark fringe shadowing her large eyes and small, pensive face.

(*right*) Jeanne Renouart, the famous Parisian actress, was painted by Vuillard in her loge, wearing a green and orange tulle dress daringly held by one shoulder strap and with her fair hair marcel-waved over her forehead.

(*right*) Norma Shearer's pure features became famous in the days of *The Student Prince*, but in spite of her essentially contemporary looks she has been cast in such historical roles as Marie Antoinette and Juliet.

(*below*) The oriental beauty of Anna May Wong's sad face made a great impact on the public when she appeared on the silent screen. Her broad cheek bones and wide apart eyes gain added charm from her thick straight fringe, which was much copied by her Western admirers.

Western Magic

*The film grows up, the movies have become
the talkies and the photographer increasingly usurps
the functions of the artist.*

(*left*) This photograph of Lee Miller, now Mrs. Roland Penrose, was taken by Manray at the time when her appearance in Cocteau's film *Le Sang d'un Poète* had set all Paris talking about her.

(*below*) Art takes a hand in altering the human form, and Modigliani painted this nude about 1917. But the model is ten years ahead of her time, for hers is the slim figure admired in the 'twenties, but never associated with the heyday of Poiret.

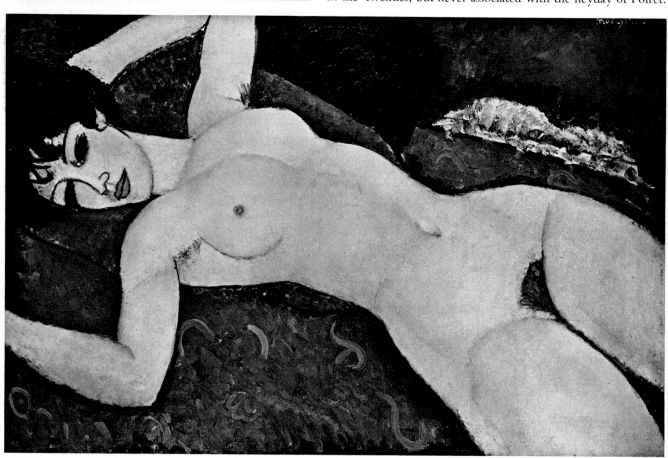

Marlene Dietrich had her first great success in *Blue Angel* and for the last quarter of a century we have been entranced by her husky voice and her sleepy eyes. To-day she continues to draw huge crowds whenever she sings in night-clubs all over the world, but only seldom appears on the screen.

The Smooth Side Parting

Fashion becomes standardised and no woman would dare appear except with her hair parted on the side, brushed and burnished smoothly

(*above*) The Lady Louis Mountbatten was born Edwina Ashley, daughter of Baron Mount Temple and granddaughter of Sir Edgar Cassel, from whom she inherited a fortune. She has always played an active part in the strenuous career of her husband and as the last Vicereine of India charmed Mr. Nehru and other Indian leaders so much that they are still her friends.

(*right*) Shining gold hair and a perfect profile and figure distinguished Doris Delavigne. She was one of the most famous beauties of the 'twenties and married Lord Castlerosse, the eccentric Irish peer whose column in Lord Beaverbrook's newspapers was a landmark in modern English journalism.

(*right*) The new importance of the bare back is illustrated by Sylvia Ashley, who became Mrs. Douglas Fairbanks, senior. Later she married Lord Stanley of Alderley and then Clark Gable. She is now Princess Djerjazde and lives in California.

ERRATUM

(*above*) "June," the former Lady Inverclyde, is Mrs. Edward Hillman and lives in Beverly Hills, California. She is now a professional artist in oil-colors and a member of the Society of Western Artists in San Francisco.

The publisher regrets that the photograph was mislabeled and is happy to note that the caption is in error.

(*right*) Dorothy Dickson was born in America and scored a tremendous success in London musicals, particularly in *Dancing Times*. She is the mother of pretty Dot Hyson, who left the stage when she married the actor Anthony Quayle.

181

The Broad,
Bare Brow

(*below*) Dolores del Rio's smooth Spanish beauty coupled with her undoubted acting ability first brought her recognition when she played the young mother in *Resurrection*, which was voted one of the best pieces of screen-acting of its year. She lives in Mexico where she has recently completed a new film.

(*above*) Nush, the wife of Eluard, the French surrealist poet, died when still very young. Here she is photographed by Manray with her lovely profile faintly reflected in her mirror.

A madonna-like serenity is
admired and dark hair
is once again drawn back
to reveal smooth foreheads

(*above*) The famous daughter of a famous mother, Eve Curie
inherited much of her parent's scientific genius but allied it
to a rare and distinguished beauty. After a successful career
in journalism she married Henri Labouisse and is now actively
associated with the work of UNRWA in the Middle East.

(*above*) A wide bare forehead is now admired and the girl in
Derain's painting has features similar to those of Eve Curie.

183

The fashion for jazz reached its high spot when Josephine Baker became the rage of Paris. Her streamlined torso was the ideal of the time and her immense vivacity and tireless energy drew crowds to whichever theatre or nightclub she appeared in. Her costumes were fabulously fantastic but Domergue preferred to paint her in the nude.

Exotic Glamour

Dark eyebrows clearly pencilled
Dark hair severely disciplined

(*right*) The enormous liquid eyes of the Princess of Kapurthala and the serenity of her brow are accentuated by the small caste mark on her forehead. She caused a sensation when she first appeared in the West and has remained a well-known example of the legendary and exotic beauty of Indian women.

(*above*) Penelope Dudley-Ward, lovely daughter of a famous beauty in the Prince of Wales's set, was one of the first society girls to appear in films. She soon, however, abandoned the screen for marriage, but remained in the world of the cinema for she is now the wife of the producer Sir Carol Reed.

(*right*) Tamara Toumanova, the famous ballet dancer, photographed by Hoyningen-Huene, dispenses with all extraneous aids to beauty and wears a costume which hides her hair but shows to advantage her large dark eyes. Her first great success was in *Cotillon*, followed by *Symphonie Fantastique*.

The Arched
Eyebrow

(*above*) Wide blue eyes beneath high arching brows and smooth blonde hair characterize the Hon. Mrs. Bryan Guinness, now the wife of Sir Oswald Mosley, leader of the British Fascist movement. She is one of a family famous for its lovely daughters; the Duchess of Devonshire and Nancy Mitford, the well-known writer, are her sisters. William Acton made this drawing not long before he died.

(*left*) Vivien Leigh had an immediate success and her beauty took London by storm when she appeared in *The Mask of Virtue* in 1933. She has since played both on stage and screen with equal facility, and has enchanted audiences the world over. Perhaps her most memorable role was Scarlett in *Gone with the Wind*. She married Sir Laurence Olivier in 1940.

(*right*) Greta Garbo is a legend in her life-time. Far more than her acknowledged beauty, her personality created a mystique which made every spectator part of the drama he witnessed, and those who saw her in *Camille* and *Queen Christina* experienced an unforgettable emotion. Hoyningen-Huene took this wonderful and hitherto unpublished photograph of her.

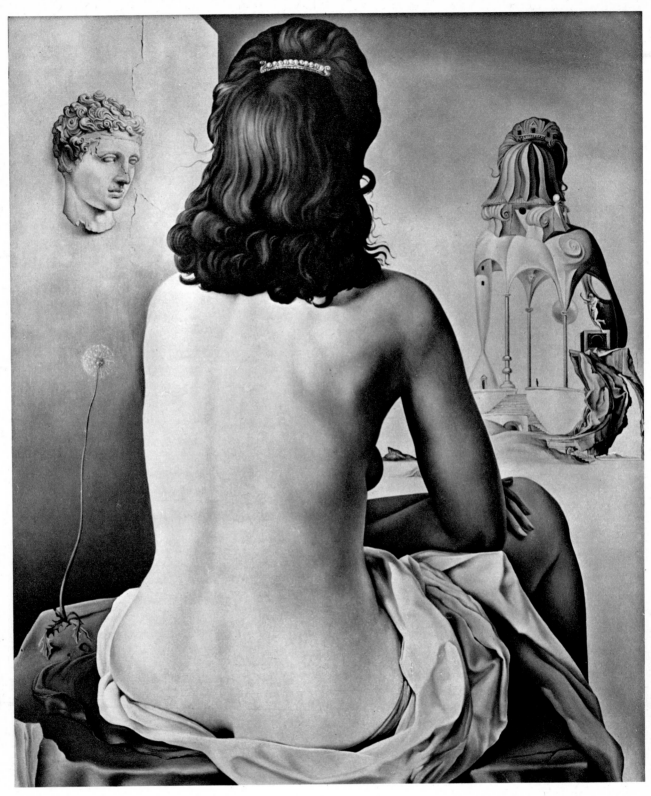

Amidst the fantasy of his painting Salvador Dali clearly shows the coiffure of the day—long curls which rest on the shoulders but front hair turned back to make a pompadour held by a comb.

The Long Bob

Hair is allowed to grow until it reaches the shoulders, permanent waving makes possible a curly frame for all faces, but the forehead remains bare.

(*above*) Veronica Lake started the peek-a-boo hair style in the 'thirties, but later cut off her hair because so many factory girls who copied her got their long locks caught in machinery. It was said the accident rate promptly went down by as much as 22 per cent. She starred in *I Married a Witch* and played with great success opposite Alan Ladd in *This Gun for Hire*.

(*left*) Jill Furse was the wife of Lawrence Whistler, the distinguished poet and engraver on glass and brother of the artist Rex Whistler. She was much admired both as an actress and a writer and her early death was mourned by many.

The Pensive Thirties

(*above*) With hair and dress alight with *paillettes*, Lady Elizabeth Paget gazes into the cracked mirror in this imaginative photograph taken by Cecil Beaton not long before she married Raimund von Hofmansthal, son of the famous poet.

(*right*) Princess Natalie Paley married couturier Lucien Lelong in the early 'thirties, when her pale moonbeam loveliness was perfectly set off by the light colours then in vogue. Later she married John Wilson, the successful theatrical producer.

A natural waistline and
more elaborate coiffures
and clothes make a tentative
but brief reappearance

(*above*) The strange, slightly oriental beauty of Florence, wife
of the brilliant young conductor Constant Lambert, lent itself
well to the increasing tendency towards decorative fashions
noticeable in the late 'thirties. Photograph by Cecil Beaton.

(*left*) Millicent Rogers came of a well-known American
family with connections in many European countries. Her
pale clear features and dark blue eyes were photographed
by Horst. She married Count Salm and died three years ago.

Present Perspective

After a world crisis during which women were regimented for the first time since the legendary Amazons, there is a reaction to extreme femininity. The waist, ignored for a quarter of a century, is nipped by "waspies" or "waist-cinchers" like the brief corsets worn by ancient Minoan women. Numerous stiff and frilly petticoats hold out full skirts and add to the illusion of smallness, while every device is used to accentuate the breasts. These, though covered, are so clearly visible beneath skin-tight sweaters that cleavage becomes a word of international significance. The décolletage is as extreme as ever it has been and barely stops short at the breastline, while on the beaches the two-piece bikini, identical to that worn one thousand five hundred years ago under the Roman Empire, scandalises the first spectators but soon becomes generally accepted.

Hair is controlled into soft waves which frame the face and neck, but the permanent curl is no longer ubiquitous and soon long straggling locks appear. Picasso paints Sylvette with a pony-tail and Juliette Greco is the ideal of the

192

Existentialist cafés. It is essential to be casual, princesses and film stars are photographed in shirt sleeves, shorts or considerably less, and the bare-foot Contessa is acclaimed a beauty. Hair becomes nibbled into a few short strands, eyes are now the dominant  feature and, remarkably like those of their Egyptian prototypes, slant perceptibly upwards beneath thickened and accentuated eyebrows. As the eyes darken and become more important, lipstick fades and the mouth becomes paler and rouge must never be noticed. The fetish of health is everywhere acknowledged, the skin must glow, the hair gleam with its own vitality – the charms of the invalid are not for this age.

We become used to 3D in technicolor; square dancing and rock 'n' roll revolutionise ballrooms and dance-halls the world over; the Ballet has enormous influence and young girls wear the flat shoes and walk with the easy movements of dancers, from whom they have borrowed their practice tights. The female form, although covered, is now revealed thigh-high and this not only within doors, where at long last contemporary design has triumphed.

But now a more formal type of woman begins to appear. Hair is carefully brushed, if short into easy waves, if long into a smooth knot set rather high at the back of the head. Ears are universally exposed and hung with ear-rings, and long necks the object of particular admiration. There is talk of skirts being both tight and long, the waist is no longer pinched, the bosom less emphasised. Will "the lady", ignored these twenty years, stage a come-back? Will she abandon the youthful casual comfort of the early 'fifties?

193

These three sisters are descendants of Pamela Fitzgerald (see p. 110) and Cecil Beaton has grouped them in imitation of Sargent's painting of their mother and aunts (see p. 150). They are the daughters of Captain and Mrs. Wyndham-Quin: in the centre is Lady Cranborne, on the right Lady Roderic Pratt and on the left Mrs. John Wyndham, who now lives at Petworth, the family house.

The marriage of Marina, the youngest daughter of Prince Nicholas of Greece, to the Duke of Kent was one of the great royal occasions of the 'thirties. Only a few years later, however, the young Duchess was left tragically widowed when the Duke was killed in a wartime air crash. The Duchess of Kent is to-day as much admired in her adopted country for her elegance and taste as for her distinguished beauty.

Beauty
in the Bone

(*above*) The lovely, severe face of Maria Casares, the French actress, is capable of every extreme of emotion and her voice is of exceptional flexibility. To have seen her in *Marie Tudor* or *L'Ennemi* by Julien Green is an unforgettable experience.

(*right*) This portrait of Mrs. Christie Miller by Annigoni contrasts her pale face and fair hair against the background of a huge black hat and dress. Her perfect Cupid's bow of a mouth appears to be smiling slightly and belies the dreamy expression of her large clear eyes with their lightly pencilled brows.

The fine contours of
cheek-bone and chin are set off by
severely disciplined hair

(*above*) Michèle Morgan, one of the great stars of the French cinema, was discovered in the 'thirties and entranced all who saw her in *Symphonie Pastorale* where her pale poetic looks harmonised perfectly with that strange film.

(*left*) One of the loveliest young women in Paris until recently was Lisa Fonssagrives. Her high cheek-bones, up-slanting eyes and arched eyebrows made her the idol of every painter and photographer. Since her marriage to the American photographer Penn, she has lived in New York.

Luxuriant Locks
Blonde or Brunette

Luxuriant hair, curled and sometimes tumbling to the shoulders, fine eyes beneath strong brows and wide, generous mouths distinguish these beauties from three different countries.

(*above*) Valerie Hobson's typically English beauty brought her early success on the screen. She is now the wife of John Profumo, and takes an active interest in politics.

(*left*) Princess Nilaufer of Hyderabad comes from one of the most fabulously wealthy families of the world. A cloud of dark hair surrounds her small head and her slender neck and shoulders emerge from a froth of tulle.

The daughter of an Argentine Ambassador to the Court of St. James's, Ana Carcano married into the English branch of one of the great American families and is now Mrs. J. J. Astor.

The Whittled Waist

Feminine graces return and are cherished:
the hand-span waist is accentuated
by billowing clouds of tulle.

(*above*) The figure returns: Mrs. Nigel Campbell, better known to her admirers as Barbara Goalen, shows the modern silhouette to be as definite as any in the past. It whittles the waist and follows the lines of the body.

(*below*) Fiona Campbell-Walter was the most beautiful debutante of her year and for a time was one of London's leading models, for her wide apart eyes and exquisite features make her extremely photogenic. She is now married to the Swiss millionaire, Baron Thyssen.

Princess Margaret on her twenty-first birthday: a special photograph taken by Cecil Beaton in Buckingham Palace. Her oval face is softly framed by her hair and she wears an exquisite organza dress which emphasises her tiny waist by its full spreading skirt.

Dark Magic

Dark curls, windblown or disciplined, and heavy eyebrows arching high above dreaming eyes are common to these slender beauties from three different countries for two of whom a photographer and painter vie with each other to produce fantastical and romantic backgrounds.

(*above*) Anne Gunning represents Irish beauty at its best. She is a descendant of the two lovely Gunning sisters who were so much admired in the eighteenth century (see pp. 94 and 95) and Richard Dormer has photographed her romantically beside an Irish lough accompanied by a huge Irish wolfhound.

(*below*) An English export to Hollywood, Elizabeth Taylor's small face and large eyes were first admired in *National Velvet*. She was one of the originators of the fashion for the heavily-defined eyebrow. Her first marriage was to the English cinema actor Michael Wilding but she is now the wife of the ebullient *Round the World in Eighty Days* Mike Todd.

(*above*) Kay Kendall's parents were a famous dance-team and she herself began in the chorus when very young, but she found her métier in the films and after a great success in the English comedy *Genevieve* went to star in Hollywood. She recently married Rex Harrison who is still playing the bewildered professor in *My Fair Lady* with his usual urbanity.

(*right*) Maria Felix scored a great success in *Maclovia*, a film set in her native Mexico, whose fire and violence is echoed by her vitality and flashing good looks. She has recently completed another Mexican film called *Hidden Beauty*. Her portrait in fantastical attire is by the Italian painter Leonor Fini.

203

(*above*) The adjective most often applied to Ava Gardner is vibrant, and those who know her say her chief characteristic is her splendid and tireless physique allied to unchanging good humour. She needs, and uses, little or no make-up and her flawless features are admirably adapted to the screen, where perhaps her greatest success has been in *Bhowani Junction*.

(*left*) Audrey Hepburn came round the door of success in 1954 and launched an altogether new type of beauty: a wistful waif, large-eyed, short-haired, minus all aids to beauty. It was Colette's sharp eyes which first discerned her possibilities and after only a few minutes acquaintanceship offered her the name-part in the Broadway adaptation of her novel *Gigi*. Shortly afterwards Audrey Hepburn's exquisite lost look made her a star on the screen in *Roman Holiday*.

Long Hair
and Straggling

(*above*) Anna Magnani's strength and magnetism have made her one of the most interesting actresses of the last decade. The magic of her large eyes shadowed by a tangle of dark hair is exquisitely portrayed by Leonor Fini.

(*left*) Juanita Forbes is an English girl with a Spanish name and looks. Here she is painted by Annigoni, whose success as a portrait painter in the last few years has made him a fortune. He has described her as his most beautiful model and this portrait was one of those which helped to establish his fame.

Hair is allowed to grow long
and hang uncurled upon the shoulders
and sometimes shadows the forehead
with a wispy fringe

(*below*) Picasso's famous portrait of Sylvette does a good deal to explain the student and teen-age craze for the pony-tail.

(*above*) Although Leslie Caron looks like an impish school-girl in this photograph by Tony Armstrong-Jones, with her long hair hanging down her back, she is the wife of producer Peter Hall and has many rôles to her credit, on stage and screen.

Short
and Nibbled

All apparent coquetry is
dispensed with and nothing but
a few short stray locks are allowed
to appear on young foreheads

(*above*) The pure oval of Ivy Nicholson's face is undisturbed
by any hair other than a wisp on the forehead: interest is
centred in the up-curved eyes and heavy eyebrows.

(*right*) Elsa Martinelli, with her expressive dark eyes, is
typical of the unkempt *gamines* who have been a recent Italian
export. She began her career as a photographic model but
soon she made her way to Hollywood where she won a prize
in a film competition. In *Manuela* she plays opposite Trevor
Howard for the first time and the rôle gives considerable
scope to her carefree, high-spirited acting.

(*right*) Suzanne Flon cut her hair to the correct military length when she played Joan of Arc in Anouilh's *l'Alouette*, **and so** helped to launch a fashion. She played in *The Little Hut* in Paris and had a great success on the screen in *Moulin Rouge*, though she prefers playing in the theatre to making films.

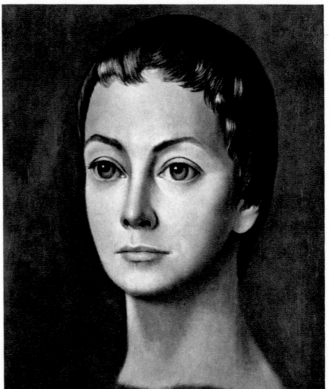

(*above*) Antony Devas used Mrs. Hugo Philipps, the lovely daughter-in-law of authoress Rosamond Lehman, as his model for this picture entitled *At the Couturier*.

(*right*) Brigitte Bardot, known as the "Modern Venus de Milo", studied ballet as a child in France and had a resounding success in *Mademoiselle Striptease* and in *Woman was Created*. Her gaiety and natural good looks devoid of all artificiality, and her radiant health, make her the contemporary ideal.

209

The Casual Life

Princesses appear, like Venus, out of the sea,
and Prime Ministers' wives lie on hay stooks;
tiaras and trains have vanished, formality has
given way to natural ease.

(*above*) Indicative of the informality now in vogue is this charming photograph by Cecil Beaton of Clarissa Churchill, a cousin of Sir Winston and the wife of Sir Anthony Eden.

(*left*) A delightfully informal outdoor photograph by Cecil Beaton shows Pandora and Atalanta, two of the three beautiful daughters of Sir Bede Clifford and his American wife.

(*right*) Unlike the princesses shown in the earlier chapters of this book, Grace Kelly, now Princess Grace of Monaco, elects to be photographed by Howell Conant with no adornment other than drops of glittering sea-water on her cheek.

The Dark Dominant Eye

(*above*) Natasha Parry is of Russian-Greek-British extraction and an actress of delicate charm. She is now the wife of the brilliant theatrical producer Peter Brook. Tony Armstrong-Jones took this telling photograph of her dark good looks.

(*right*) Among Pier Angeli's chief successes on the films are *Port Afrique* and *Star of Tomorrow*. She is married to Vic Damone, and once, when they were parted for a month, they spent over five hundred pounds on telephone calls.

No contrivances of coiffure
detract from the importance of
these expressive eyes
accentuated by dark brows

(*above*) Beriosova's fluttering pale charm was seen to great advantage in *The Phantom* and her dancing in the *Prince of the Pagodas* was a revelation even to her most enthusiastic admirers. She seems capable of expressing every shade of emotion.

(*left*) The Viscountess Hambledon comes of a distinguished Roman family and Antony Devas has successfully captured her statuesque beauty in this head and shoulders portrait which was exhibited at the Royal Academy in 1956.

Countess Dolores von Fuerstenberg married her step-brother and became Mrs. Patrick Guinness when she was only nineteen. One of her many claims to beauty is her swan-like neck, exquisitely recorded in this photograph by Richard Avedon.

The Long Neck

Three contemporary examples
of an attribute which has always
received great admiration

(*above*) Mrs. Michael Severn is the eldest child of Madame Fitzgerald, whose Irish title allows her to be called "Madame" with no suffix, and who has transmitted the legendary beauty of the family to her daughter who now lives in London.

(*left*) Bouché's clever pencil has caught the essence of Audrey Hepburn's elfin charm and stresses her slender neck and the heavily pencilled eyebrows which shadow her large eyes.

Airs without
Artifice

*The new young beauties of the late 'fifties
are not in bondage to the past but live uncluttered
by contrivances, unfettered by tradition.*

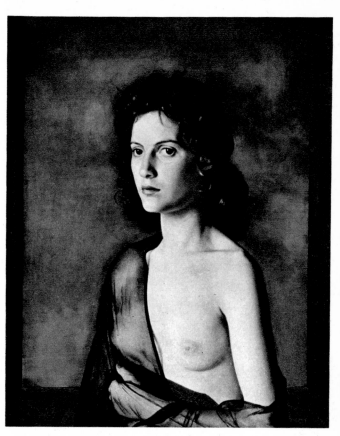

(*above*) Alert and self-confident, *La Belle Italienne*, painted by
Annigoni, allows her hair to curl naturally on to her slender
shoulders and uses no exaggerated maquillage.

(*above*) The Danish Charlotte Bergsoe's long red hair contrasts admirably with her lovely fair skin and sparkling blue
eyes. She is the daughter of Countess Ahfeldt Laurvig and
her godfather is Prince Axel of Denmark.

(*below*) Nude on the beach. A photograph which repeats
with remarkable fidelity the painting by Couture on page 130
and illustrates the out-of-doors life which is the ideal but not
the lot of the present day girl.

Heather Sears is a new name in the theatre but already she has made an impact
on both stage and screen and has played with Joan Crawford in *The Story of
Esther Costello*. She adds the spice of humour to her intelligent good looks.

Where do we go from here?

Will the gamine continue on her free and easy way? or will a change of fashion make ladies of us all?

(*above*) Princess Ira Fuerstenberg, daughter of Prince Tassilo and Princess Clara von Fuerstenberg, caused a sensation when she modelled clothes in a Florentine dress show when little more than fifteen. She married Prince von Hohenlohe when still only sixteen and now lives in Mexico.

(*left*) Anita Ekberg is of Scandinavian descent and scored a great success as Elena Kouraguine in the screen version of Tolstoy's *War and Peace*. She is married to Anthony Steel.

(*right*) Four studies of Miss Marilyn Monroe: for the filmgoer she has become the personification of sex and her 'vital statistics' are the ideal of two continents. Recently, however, she has starred with Sir Laurence Olivier and has married the well-known playwright Arthur Miller.

ACKNOWLEDGEMENTS

I record my thanks to the following for permission to reproduce the pictures in this book. M.G.

TITLE PAGE Three Graces: *Fresco from Pompeii* National Museum, Naples. *Raphael* Musée Condé, Chantilly (Photo: Mansell collection). *Dürer* (Photo: Mansell collection). *Rubens* Prado, Madrid (Photo: Mansell collection). *Boucher* Louvre, *Renoir* Charles Laughton collection (Photo: Tisne). *Picasso* Rex Nankivell collection (Photo: Arts Council, London)

CONTENTS

PAGE 6 *Prehistoric Statuette* R. Sainsbury collection

7 *Mexican Statuette* reproduced from *l'Oeuil* (Photo: Robert Doisneau). *Portrait de Mme X* by Carolus-Duran Musée de Luxembourg, Paris

8 *Lady of Elche* Prado Museum, Madrid

9 *Head* Villa Giulia, Rome (Photo: Mercury, Milan)

10 *Lady curling her fringe* and *Doe-Eyed Dancer* (Photos: Mansell collection)

11 *Miniature fresco* and *Ladies in Blue* (Photos: Ashmolean Museum, Oxford)

12 *Minoan Court Lady* and *The Lady of Sports* Candia Museum, Crete (Photo: Mansell collection)

13 *Pottery figures* (Photos: Ashmolean Museum, Oxford)

14 *Limestone Goddess* Metropolitan Museum, New York

15 *Queen Nefertiti* Berlin Museum (Photo: Mansell collection): Cairo Museum (Photo: Hirmer Verlag, Munich)

16 *Wife of Rameses' brother* (Photo: Hirmer Verlag, Munich)

17 *Queen Hatshepsut* Metropolitan Museum, New York

18 *Detail from the Ludovisi relief of Persephone* Terme Museum, Rome (Photo: Mansell collection). *Kore* (Photo: Seraf, Athens)

19 *Kneeling Venus* Rhodes Museum and *Aspasia* Berlin Museum (Photos: Mansell collection)

20 *Aphrodite* Cyprus Museum and *Phryne* by Praxiteles, Berlin Museum

21 *Phryne* by Praxiteles (Photo: by permission of Charles Seltman). *Venus de Milo* Louvre, Paris

22 *Girl putting on a shoe* Bally Shoe Museum, Zurich

23 *Pottery Jug* (Photo: Mansell collection). *Terracotta Head* Louvre, Paris (Photo: Bulloz)

24 *Girls Gossiping* British Museum, London. *Girls Gossiping* (Photo: Herbert List, Munich). *Tanagra Figure* Louvre, Paris

25 *Mother and Daughter* Sardinia (Photo: Mansell collection). *Tanagra Figure* Louvre, Paris. *Three Tanagra Figures* Private collection, Paris (Photos: Herbert List, Munich)

26 *Agrippina Minor* (Photo: Darma). *Poppaea* Private collection, London. *False Curls* Capitoliano Museum, Rome

27 *Egypto-Roman portrait* (Photo: Mansell collection)

28 *The Writer* Casa di Libanio, Italy (Photo: Mansell collection)

PAGE 29 *Bikinis* Syracuse Museum, Italy (Photos: Fontana, reproduced by permission of Professor G. V. Gentili)

30 *Detail from Mosaic* St. Vitale, Ravenna, Italy (Photo: Arts Council, London)

31 *Galla Placidia* Brescia Museum, Italy (Photo: Mercurio, Milan)

32 *St. Agnes* St. Apollinare, Ravenna, Italy (Photo: Arts Council, London). *Salome* St. Mark's, Venice (Photo: Mansell collection). *Byzantine Lady* (Photo: Alinari)

33 *Antonius and Joanna* and *Theodora* San Vitale, Ravenna, Italy (Photos: U. Trapani, Ravenna, Italy and Arts Council, London)

34 *La Dame à la Licorne* and *A Mon Seul Désir* Cluny Museum, Paris (Photos: Victoria and Albert Museum, London)

35 *Duc de Berry's Calendar* by Pol de Limbourg, Bibliothèque Nationale, Paris. *St. Catherine* by Crivelli, Brera Museum, Milan. *Marcia*, Bibliothèque Nationale, Paris

36 *Mermaid* Bibliothèque Nationale, Paris. *Judgement of Paris* Museum of Art, Basle. *Lady combing her hair* Angers Museum, France (Photo: Victoria and Albert Museum)

37 *Hippolyte* by Carpaccio, Jacqmart-André Museum, Paris (Photo: Bulloz)

38 *Ariadne* and *Three Muses dancing* Bibliothèque Nationale, Paris

39 *The Charm of Love* by Mittlerheinischer Meister, Leipzig Museum

40 *Fragment of Statuette* Havre Museum, France (Photo: Knoll, Leipzig, reproduced by courtesy of 'Verve'). *Virgin* Notre Dame, Toulouse (Photo: Bibliothèque Nationale, Paris)

41 *Virgin* Toledo Cathedral, Spain. *Uta* Nuremberg Cathedral, Germany (Photo: Helga Schmidt-Glassner). *Margaret of France* Lincoln Cathedral, England (Photo: Record and General Ltd.)

42 *Portrait* by Petrus Christus, Berlin Museum. *Young Flemish Woman* by Rogier van der Weyden, National Gallery, London (Photo: Mansell collection)

43 *Princess of Trebizond* by Pisanello, St. Anastasia's Church, Verona, Italy (Photo: Mansell collection). *Bathsheba* by Memling, Staatsgalerie, Stuttgart

44 *Detail of St. Peter and St. Dorothy* by the Master of Bartholomew, National Gallery, London

45 *Sleeping Venus* by Giorgione, Dresden Museum, Germany

46 *Venus Rising from the Sea* by Botticelli, Uffizi Gallery, Florence, Italy and *Girl* by Botticelli, Frankfurt Museum (Photos: Mansell collection)

47 *Head of Flora* and *The Three Graces* by Botticelli, Uffizi Gallery, Florence, Italy (Photos: Mansell collection)

48 *Siennese Girls* by Neroccio de' Landi, National Gallery, Washington

220

221

223

PRINTED IN GREAT BRITAIN BY CLARKE AND SHERWELL LTD., NORTHAMPTON